Political Agendas for Education

From the Religious Right to the Green Party

Third Edition

Sociocultural, Political, and Historical Studies in Education
Joel Spring, Editor

Political Agendas for Education

From the Religious Right to the Green Party

Third Edition

Joel Spring
Queens College
City University of New York

Routledge
Taylor & Francis Group
New York   London

Routledge is an imprint of the
Taylor & Francis Group, an informa business

Cover design by Kathryn Houghtaling Lacey

Library of Congress Cataloging-in-Publication Data

Spring, Joel H.
Political agendas for education : from the religious right to the
green party / Joel Spring—3rd ed.
p.   cm.
Includes bibliographical references and index.
ISBN 0-8058-5256-5 (cloth : alk. paper)
ISBN 0-8058-5257-3 (pbk. : alk. paper)
1. Politics and education—United States. 2. Liberal-
ism—United States. 3. Conservatism—United States. I. Title.
II. Series.

LC89.S663 2005
379.73—dc22   2005040016
                                                               CIP

First Published by Lawrence Erlbaum Associates, Inc., Publishers
10 Industrial Avenue
Mahwah, New Jersey 07430

Reprinted 2008 by Routledge

Routledge
Taylor and Francis Group
270 Madison Avenue
New York, NY 10016

Routledge
Taylor and Francis Group
2 Park Square
Milton Park, Abingdon
Oxon OX14 4RN

Printed in the United States of America
10 9 8 7 6 5 4 3 2

Contents

Preface

The 2004 presidential campaign and No Child Left Behind Act of 2001 are the focus of this Third Edition of *Political Agendas for Education*. No Child Left Behind is a legislative compromise that includes parts of the educational agendas of compassionate conservatives, neoconservatives, and New Democrats. During the 2004 presidential campaign, Ralph Nader's presidential organization and the Green Party criticized the testing and standards requirements of the legislation.

In this edition, I will discuss the ideological perspective of each major political group and how its ideology is represented in No Child Left Behind. In chapter 1, I discuss the ideology of Republicans who identify themselves as compassionate conservatives and how their religious agenda appears in the legislation. Chapter 2 deals with the ideology of Republicans identified as neoconservative and how their free market ideas are represented in No Child Left Behind. New Democrats, who claim a major responsibility for the passage of No Child Left Behind and who support the accountability requirements of the legislation, are discussed in chapter 3. The educational agendas and criticisms of No Child Left Behind by Ralph Nader's 2004 presidential campaign organization, as well as the Green Party, the Rainbow Coalition, and the National Organization of Women are analyzed in chapter 4. And finally, chapter 5 provides a chart comparing the educational concerns of each political faction.

Compassionate Conservatism and No Child Left Behind: The Republican Educational Agenda for the 21st Century

"Let me tell you what I think the bill says," President George W. Bush explained in defending the No Child Left Behind Act of 2001. "I believe that our society must believe every child can learn, and that means we've set high standards ... I've heard it all—we can't test, we test too much. We test too much. See, all you do is teach to test. Listen, if you can teach a child to read, they can pass a test."[1]

The No Child Left Behind Act of 2001 embodies a half century of Republican hopes for changing American schools, including support of standards, testing, school choice, character education, and school prayer, and opposition to bilingual education, multicultural education, and gay rights. The ideological underpinnings of No Child Left Behind are compassionate conservatism and neoconservativism. "Compassionate conservatism," President Bush asserts, "places great hope and confidence in public education. Our economy depends on higher and higher skills, requiring every American to have the basic tools of learning. Every public school should be the path of upward mobility."[2]

In this chapter, I will explain how compassionate conservative ideology is embodied in No Child Left Behind. In chapter 2, I will discuss the neoconservative underpinnings to the legislation. As a guide to this discussion, I have provided below a list of the major sections of No Child Left Behind. I must warn the reader that these are only what I consider to be important parts of the massive 670 pages that makeup the legislation. Stuck among the verbiage of the law are many other educational mandates. I will be referring to this list as I discuss the Republican agenda for education.

Highlights of the No Child Left Behind Act of 2001

1. Title I—Improving the Academic Achievement of the Disadvantaged
   a. Requires state to establish academic standards for mathematics, reading, language arts, and science.
   b. By the 2005-06 school year, states must begin testing students in Grades 3–8 annually in reading and mathematics. By 2007-08, they must test students in science at least once in elementary, middle, and high school. The tests must be aligned with state academic standards.
   c. A sample of fourth and eighth graders in each state must also participate in the National Assessment of Educational Progress testing program in reading and math every other year.
   d. If a school receiving federal Title I funding fails to achieve adequate yearly progress 2 years in a row, it must be provided technical assistance and its students must be offered a choice of other public schools to attend. Students in schools that fail to make adequate progress 3 years in a row must also be offered supplemental educational services, including private tutoring. For continued failures, a school would be subject to outside corrective measures, including possible governance changes.
   e. Beginning in the 2002-2003 school year, states and local school districts are to disseminate report cards that are understandable to parents and provide information on student achievement.
   f. The act creates a program called Reading First, funded at $1.02 billion in 2004, to help states and districts set up "scientific, research-based" reading programs for children in Grades K–3 (with priority given to high-poverty areas).
2. Title II creates a new program called "Teaching of Traditional American History." Grants are be awarded under the program to promote the teaching of traditional American history separate from social studies and as a distinct academic subject in elementary and secondary schools.
3. Title V—Promoting Informed Parental Choice and Innovative Programs
   a. Provides funds to state and local governments to support parental choice of schools.
   b. Partnerships in Character Education section of Title V provides funds for integrating secular character education into curricula and teaching methods of schools.
4. English Language Acquisition, Language Enhancement, and Academic Achievement Act
   a. Changes the original political goals of bilingual education as symbolized by the renaming of the "Office of Bilingual Educa-

tion and Minority Languages Affairs" to "Office of English Language Acquisition, Language Enhancement, and Academic Achievement for Limited."
    b. Emphasis on English acquisition in contrast to maintaining languages of conquered peoples (Native American, Puerto Rican, and Pacific Islanders).
5. Boy Scouts of America Equal Access Act
    a. Requires schools to allow Boy Scouts to use its facilities. Many schools banned the use of school facilities because the Boy Scouts discriminated against gay youth.
6. School Prayer section of the legislation gives the U.S. Department of Education an active role in ensuring that school districts allow for school prayer within the boundaries of the law and it requires local school districts to certify in writing that they do not prevent or interfere with participation in constitutionally protected prayer.
7. In general, the legislation supports privatization of public school services.[3]

COMPASSIONATE CONSERVATISM

A compassionate conservative ideology can be used to justify most of No Child Left Behind, particularly sections on "Partnerships in Character Education" and "School Prayer." Briefly stated, compassionate conservatism assumes that in most cases poverty, crime, and problems facing a democratic society are a result of a failure in personal character and values. Consequently, direct charity or government welfare doesn't solve the problem; in fact, it might reinforce negative character traits. The solution is providing the conditions by which people can help themselves. Self-help, compassionate conservatives believe, will result in a transformation of character and the acquisition of positive values. This character transformation is aided by exposure to religious values. Consequently, the imposed discipline of educational standards and testing is to help students, according to compassionate conservatives, to develop the character traits of self-discipline and hard work. Aiding in this process are character education, student-initiated school prayer, and exposure to religious values.

The importance of values was emphasized by George W. Bush when, as governor of Texas, he wrote that, "*Dream and the Nightmare* by Myron Magnet crystallized for me the impact the failed culture of the sixties had on our values and society. It helped create dependency on government, undermine family and eroded values which had stood the test of time and which are critical if we want a decent and hopeful tomorrow for every single American."[4] Myron Magnet was editor of the ultraconservative Manhattan Institute's *City Journal* and former member of the editorial board of *Fortune* magazine. He considers the 1960s and early 1970s the cultural watershed of American history. During this period American values, he argued, deteriorated as a result of a cultural revolution led "by an elite of opinion makers, policymakers, and mythmakers—lawyers, judges, professors, political staffers, journalists, writers, TV and movie honchos, clergymen—and it was overwhelmingly a liberal, left-of-center elite."[5] Out of this cultural revolution, according to Magnet, emerged a whole host of programs, including the War on Poverty, court-ordered busing, Affirmative Action, drug treatment programs, and the political correctness movement at colleges.

Most important, Magnet argues, the cultural revolution overturned the traditional American values that supported hard work and family life as the basis for economic success and good living. The new values were represented by two "epochal" expressions. The first was the sexual revolution, which Magnet feels resulted in increased divorce, illegitimacy, and female-headed families. The second was the 1960s counterculture that rejected an unjust economic system and hard work.

Basic to Magnet's argument is a belief that values determine the economic and social systems, as compared to the assumption that social and economic systems determine values. In other words, similar to University of Texas journalism professor Marvin Olasky, Magnet believes that the major liberal error was to try to eliminate poverty by changing the economic system as opposed to changing the values of the poor. Magnet presented the following argument:

> On the grandest level, if you believe that human choices and actions, rather than blind, impersonal forces, determine the shape of history, then the ideas and visions impelling the human actors become crucial causes of the reality that unfolds. Men don't simply have their environment handed to them from on high; they collectively make and remake it from the cultural and material resources that lie ready at hand. And great men augment those resources by inventing new techniques and new ideas.[6]

Within this framework of thinking, Magnet argues that American society advanced because of the Protestant values that promoted a free economy. Citing Max Weber, Magnet identifies these values as individualism, hard work, and a belief that success is a sign of God's blessing.

Other conservatives echo Magnet's sentiments. Pat Buchanan, the conservative political commentator and 2000 presidential candidate for the Reform Party, provided the following description of the beliefs of the religiously oriented compassionate conservatives: "Among the social conservatives [of the Republican Party] resides the Religiously-oriented compassionate conservatives to whom the expulsion of God from the classroom, the rise of the drug culture, and the 'sexual revolution' are unmistakable symptoms of cultural decadence and national decline."[7]

Also, Bush and many Republicans are influenced by the work of University of Texas journalism professor Marvin Olasky. In his office on the Austin campus, located only a short distance from the Texas state capitol building, Olasky professed the need for a rebirth of American compassion. As editor of the weekly news magazine *Christian* and as author of two important books, *The Tragedy of American Compassion* and *Renewing American Compassion,* Olasky blamed government welfare programs for worsening the moral conditions of the poor and, as a result, perpetuating poverty in the United States. Olasky's answer to helping the poor was returning welfare programs to faith-based organizations.

Influenced by Olasky's *Renewing American Compassion,* Bush proposed during his 2000 campaign, and later as President, that faith-based organizations be allowed to compete for federal funds. Regarding education, Bush proposed funding after-school activities operated by faith-based organizations. In reference to federal after-school programs of the 21st Century Community Learning Centers program originally created during the Clinton years, Bush suggested "introduc[ing] legislation to open 100 percent of the 21st Century programs funding to competitive bidding ... [to] allow youth development groups, local charities, churches, synagogues, mosques and other community and faith-based organizations to compete for these federal funds on an equal footing with schools."[8]

Federal programs operated by faith-based groups, according to Olasky and other compassionate conservatives, would ensure the teaching of traditional moral values to America's poor. To Olasky, humans are basically sinful, and their inherent sinfulness must be curbed by moral instruction. The danger of providing welfare funds without demanding work in return, he argues, is that humans can easily slip into a depraved condition. Olasky maintained that in "orthodox Christian anthropology ... man's sinful nature leads toward indolence, and that an impoverished person given a dole without obligation is likely to descend into pauperism."[9]

Reforming the government welfare system is fruitless, according to Olasky, because constitutional restrictions do not allow bureaucrats to teach religious values. The only hope, he argues, is to replace government programs with charities operated by faith-based organizations. Olasky supports his argument with a historical survey of private charities that includes the exhortation of 17th-century Puritan divine Cotton Mather: "Don't nourish [the idle] and harden'em in that, but find employment for them. Find'em work; set'em to work; keep'em to work."[10]

Olasky maintains that there are beneficial results from a direct relationship between the giver and receiver as opposed to a the relationship between a faceless government bureaucracy and the receiver. Giving, he declares, is a moral act. Personal charity provides benefits to the giver through engagement with the suffering of others. The engagement with suffering supposedly strengthens the religious faith of the giver which, in turn, results in providing a model of religious values for the recipient. Consequently, replacing government-operated welfare programs with faith-based and personal charity, according to Olasky, strengthens the general moral values of society while providing the poor with a real means of escaping poverty. Regarding the Christian definition of compassion, Olasky stated that, "The word points to personal involvement with the needy, suffering with them, not just giving to them. 'Suffering with' means adopting hard-to-place babies, providing shelter to women undergoing crisis ... working one-on-one with a single mother."[11]

Therefore, compassionate conservativism is based on the importance of ideas, as they affect values and character, in determining social conditions. Consequently, control of schools and media is important. Pat Buchanan quotes Mazzini: "Ideas rule the world and its events. A revolution is a passage of an idea from theory to practice. Whatever men say, material interests never caused and never will cause a revolution."[12] Agreeing with Buchanan, William Bennett, who served 9 years in public office as head of the National Endowment for the Humanities, as Secretary of Education under Ronald Reagan, and as drug czar under George Bush, stated that "I have come to the conclusion that the issues surrounding the culture and our values are the most important ones .... They are at the heart of our resolution of the knottiest problems of public policy, whether the subject be education, art, race relations, drugs, crime, or raising children."[13] For Bennett, the solution to public problems was teaching morality and Western cultural values.

Compassionate conservatives believe that a well-functioning democracy depends on the morality of the individual. This particular belief was prevalent among U.S. leaders during the period after the American Revolution. Revolutionary leaders believed in a concept of Christian liberty in which true freedom required a belief in God. Within this context a democratic polity can safely function only when all citizens are controlled by their belief in a common morality and culture. From this perspective, the role of public schools in a democracy is to instill Christian morality and a common culture.[14]

To support the conviction that an acceptance of Christ and Christian morality are necessary for maintaining democracy, William Bennett quotes George Washington's farewell address: "Of all the dispositions and habits which lead to political prosperity, religion and morality are indispensable supports .... And let us with caution indulge the supposition that morality can be maintained without religion."[15]

With similar language, Ralph Reed, a founder of the Christian Coalition and its first executive director, argues that democracy depends on citizens and their government showing allegiance to God. "In this greater moral context," Reed states, "faith as a political force is not undemocratic; it is the very essence of democracy."[16]

In contrast, Michael Lind, a former conservative and at present a critic of the right, argues that right-wing Republicans, such as Buchanan and Olasky, launched a cultural war against public schools as a method of diverting "the wrath of wage-earning populist voters from Wall Street and corporate America to other targets: the universities, the media, racial minorities, homosexuals, immigrants."[17] In fact, Lind referred to conservative claims of a crisis in public education as their "second great policy hoax," resulting in many Americans being persuaded that the schools are failing the nation.[18]

Although criticism of public schools, as Lind suggested, might be a distraction from the growing economic inequalities in U.S. society, no one who has sat through school board meetings or read court transcripts involving debates over sex education, school prayer, censorship of textbooks, and school choice can doubt the strong beliefs of the compassionate conservative. Drawing its support from well-organized evangelical Christians, the religiously oriented compassionate conservatives have launched a crusade to save American education and democracy.

Believing in the overriding importance of Christian morality and culture for solving social problems and maintaining democracy, the religiously oriented compassionate conservatives support school prayer, school choice, abolition of secular humanism in public schools, censorship of textbooks and books in school libraries, restricting sex education to teaching abstinence, and stopping the spread of multiculturalism.

COMPASSIONATE CONSERVATISM
AND NO CHILD LEFT BEHIND

Therefore, the character education and religious sections of No Child Left Behind directly support compassionate conservative ideology. "Character education," according to a press release from the U.S. Department of Education, "is a key feature of No Child Left Behind, the landmark education reform law designed to change the culture of American schools."[19] In 2002, the U.S. Department of Education began funding applications for character education programs under the No Child Left Behind Act (as noted in 3b of the legislative summary given previously). U.S. Secretary of Education Rod Paige announced in 2003, "We have invested nearly $24 million in character education in FY 2003 because we believe that building strong character is as essential as reading, math and science."[20]

While character education in public schools is to be secular, the Bush agenda linked it to cooperative work with faith-based organizations. Behind a poster proclaiming "Compassion in Action" at the 11th Regional White House Conference on Faith–Based and Community Initiatives, Secretary Paige declared, "With a stroke of a pen, the President signaled that this Administration will knock down any barrier, will do whatever it takes to get people of faith and goodwill involved in helping solve some of the problems in our society."[21] When John Porter was appointed U.S. Department of Education's Director of Faith-Based and Community Initiative, Secretary Paige used the language of compassionate conservativism: "John Porter is a leader in our nation's army of compassion. Some of the most successful, uplifting and effective programs to help children are run by faith-based and community organizations. We plan to utilize the hundreds of faith-based and community soldiers around the country to ensure that every child of every religion, race and ethnicity gets the best education America can offer them, and John will help guide our efforts."[22]

In July, 2004, the U.S. Department of Education issued a pamphlet describing the relationship between No Child Left Behind and faith-based organizations. The pamphlet asserts, "With No Child Left Behind, schools and religious organizations can become even more powerful allies in the effort to ensure that all children—regardless of their race, family income or the language spoken in their homes—receive a high-quality education."[23] The pamphlet describes the following opportunities for faith–based organizations to participate in No Child Left Behind:

> Faith-based organizations can receive funds to provide tutoring and other academic enrichment services for eligible low-income students. Religious organizations can become supplemental educational services providers by applying to states and then working with districts to provide services directly to students in reading language arts and mathematics.
>
> In addition to becoming supplemental educational services providers, faith-based groups can receive grants from a range of other programs that provide extra academic help.
>
> To help increase awareness and understanding of No Child Left Behind, the U.S. Department of Education provides free, user-friendly materials in English and Spanish that can strengthen the work of faith-based organizations.[24]

The pamphlet also urges clergy to talk to their congregations about No Child Left Behind and recommends that clergy and community leaders share educational success stories and information about resources available under the legislation. Clergy are called on to investigate their possible roles as service providers under the legislation and to work with local school boards and state education agencies.

THE REPUBLICAN PARTY AND THE CHRISTIAN COALITION

A great deal of the political support for compassionate conservativism comes from the Christian Coalition, which is the largest political organization representing the religiously oriented compassionate conservatives. The Christian Coalition was organized in 1989 by televangelist Pat Robertson and Ralph Reed after Pat Robertson's unsuccessful Presidential campaign in 1988. In 2001, the organization claimed a membership of more than 1.5 million, working in 1,500 chapters in all 50 states, with central headquarters located in Washington, DC. Robertson described the group as "a coalition of pro-family Roman Catholics, evangelicals, and other people of faith working together to become the unified voice of families with children in middle class America."[25]

The religiously oriented compassionate conservatives became affiliated with the Republican Party because of shifting patterns of political allegiances. In the 1970s and 1980s, Republican leaders tried to break the attachment of southern Whites and northern White ethnic groups to the Democratic Party. During the early 1970s, President Richard Nixon consciously supported Affirmative Action policies as a method of dividing the Democratic coalition of northern White union members, White ethnic groups, and minority groups. In part, the Democrats contributed to their losses by supporting Affirmative-Action hiring as opposed to race-neutral hiring. This resulted in a major realignment of parties, with many northern urban Whites flocking to the Republican camp.[26]

Also, Nixon hoped to win over traditional southern White Democrats by opposing the integration of schools by the busing of students. The traditional Democratic southern power structure was built around racist policies, including the segregation of public schools. Many Whites were alienated from the national Democratic Party because of its support of civil rights and therefore joined the Republican Party. In addition, many southern Blacks, who had traditionally viewed the Republican Party as the party of Lincoln, joined the Democratic party. Underlying these racial politics were religious politics. This combination of racial and religious politics had a profound effect on Republican policies regarding schools. After U.S. Supreme Court rulings in the 1960s prohibiting officially conducted school prayers and Bible reading, many evangelical Christians declared the public school system an enemy of Christianity and began sending their children to newly created private Christian academies. Fears of racial integration and godless classrooms resulted in the rapid growth of private Christian schools. Like Catholic parents, who thought it unfair to be taxed for support of public schools while they were paying tuition for religious schools, evangelicals demanded government support of private schools. Initiating a "school choice" movement, evangelicals argued that state and federal governments should provide financial assistance so that parents could make a choice for their children between public and private schools.[27]

Reed claimed that evangelical Christians abandoned the Democratic Party in the late 1970s when the head of the Internal Revenue Service in the Carter administration required Christian schools to prove that they were not established to preserve segregation. During the early 1970s there were rumblings that many of the Christian academies in the South were created as havens for White students fleeing integration. In Reed's words, "More than any other single episode, the IRS move against Christian schools sparked the explosion of the movement that would become known as the religious right."[28]

The use of religious politics by the Republican Party is exemplified by a 1996 interview with James Pinkerton, an advisor to the Reagan and Bush administrations and author of *What Comes Next: The End of Big Government—And the New Paradigm Ahead*. In response to a question about divisions within the Republican Party, Pinkerton replied: "Thirty years ago, Kevin Phillips, Pat Buchanan, and people like that were strategizing that we, the Republicans, win over all the southern Fundamentalists and all northern urban Catholics, and we'll build a new American majority party. And that sort of has happened. We won over a lot of urban Catholics and the South is now Republican."[29]

Responding to the same question, William Kristol, former chief of staff to Dan Quayle and editor of the *Weekly Standard,* said, "The Republicans made the right bet demographically to bet against Episcopalians, Methodists, and Presbyterians, and with Evangelicals."[30] The result of what has been called the "southernization" of the Republican Party was a split between Republicans who were primarily interested in issues regarding abortion, morality, culture, and schools and those who were primarily interested in economic issues. From the perspective of the religiously oriented compassionate conservatives, moderate Republicans were concerned with protecting the interests of big business. Reed wanted the Republican Party to become "the party of Main Street, not Wall Street." He went on to claim that "the real battle for the soul of our nation is not fought primarily over the gross national product and the prime interest rate, but over virtues, values, and the culture."[31] Echoing Reed, Buchanan rejected moderate Republican ties to business and, parodying Calvin Coolidge, said, "The business of America is not business."[32]

One leader of the so-called "electronic church," Jerry Falwell, took the concerns of the religiously oriented compassionate conservatives directly to the 1980 Republican presidential candidate, Ronald Reagan. Falwell's television program, *Old-Time Gospel Hour,* was seen in more than 12 million homes in the United States. In 1979, before meeting with Reagan, Falwell attended a lunch sponsored by the Heritage Foundation. Its director, Paul Weyrich, told him there was a "moral majority" waiting for a call to political action. Falwell jumped at the phrase and named his group the Moral Majority. Under Falwell's leadership, the organization held rallies around the country supporting the legalization of school prayer, school choice, and abolition of abortion. Within a space of 2 years, the Moral Majority had 2 million members and was raising $10 million annually.[33]

The wedding between Ronald Reagan and the Moral Majority occurred shortly after the 1980 Republican convention when Reagan was asked to address 20,000 evangelicals at a rally in Dallas. Reagan told the group, "I know that you cannot endorse me [because of the tax-exempt status of the Moral Majority], but I endorse you and everything you do."[34] Giving hope to evangelicals opposed to evolutionary theory, Reagan expressed doubts about the plausibility of Darwinian ideas. After the 1980 election, Reagan supported the religiously oriented compassionate conservatives's agenda by endorsing legislation for a tuition tax credit to allow parents to choose between public and private schools and by promising to support a school prayer amendment. After 1980, school choice and school prayer became a standard fixture in Republican platforms.

By 1996, the political power of evangelical Christians working through the Christian Coalition was a fixture in Republican politics. For instance, Presidential candidate Bob Dole wanted to focus on an economic agenda while avoiding a strong stand against abortion, but the Christian Coalition threatened to disrupt the 1996 convention unless the party platform opposed abortion. Consequently, the committee writing the Republican platform capitulated to the religiously oriented compassionate conservatives by including the following plank in the 1996 Republican Party Platform: "The unborn has a fundamental individual right to life which cannot be infringed. We support a human life amendment to the Constitution and we endorse legislation to make clear that the Fourteenth Amendment's protections apply to unborn children."[35]

The 2004 Republican Platform continues this tradition:

> As a country, we must keep our pledge to the first guarantee of the Declaration of Independence. That is why we say the unborn child has a fundamental individual right to life which cannot be infringed. We support a human life amendment to the Constitution and we endorse legislation to make it clear that the Fourteenth Amendment's protections apply to unborn children. Our purpose is to have legislative and judicial protection of that right against those who perform abortions. We oppose using public revenues for abortion and will not fund organizations which advocate it. We support the

appointment of judges who respect traditional family values and the sanctity of innocent human life.[36]

One favored method of the religiously oriented compassionate conservatives for protecting their children from the perceived anti-Christian attitudes of public schools is home schooling. For parents who cannot afford a private religious school or do not live near a religious school that meets their needs, home schooling is an important option. The 2004 Republican platform states: "As stated earlier, we applaud efforts to promote school choice initiatives that give parents more control over their children's education. By the same token, we defend the option for home schooling and call for vigilant enforcement of laws designed to protect family rights and privacy in education."[37]

Today the Christian Coalition, through its headquarters in Washington, DC, maintains close tabs on legislation. It immediately alerts its membership about any bill in Congress that is important to the interests of its members. Members are given the postal and e-mail addresses and the fax and telephone numbers of their Congressional representatives so that they can express their viewpoints on pending legislation. However, the real political activity is in local churches. This raises the issue of religious involvement in politics.

In 2004, the Christian Coalition provided the following justification for blending religion and politics. The organization's Web site states:

> We are driven by the belief that people of faith have a right and a responsibility to be involved in the world around them. That involvement includes community, social and political action. Whether on a stump, in print, over the airways the Christian Coalition is dedicated to equipping and educating God's people with the resources and information to battle against anti-family legislation.

> Since the beginning the Christian Coalition has provided critical pro-family information in order to challenge individuals, churches and community groups to make a difference at all levels of government.

> Effective citizen activism begins with knowledge—and the Christian Coalition's ability to break down the complexity of politics and convey those issues clearly with solvable opportunities is what makes our information different.[38]

The Christian Coalition also lists as its major political activities:

Our Five-Fold Mission

- Represent the pro-family point of view before local councils, school boards, state legislatures and Congress.
- Speak out in the public arena and in the media.
- Train leaders for effective social and political action.
- Inform pro-family voters about timely issues and legislation.

- Protest anti-Christianity bigotry and defend the rights of people of faith.[39]

Of course, political activity threatens the tax-exempt status of churches. Therefore, the Christian Coalition provides a carefully crafted list of do's and don'ts. In the official words of the organization, "And although a church's tax status does limit the amount of political activity it may engage in, it does not prohibit a church from encouraging citizenship."[40] The Christian Coalition informs ministers that the provided list of "do's and don'ts will help guide you, without jeopardizing your church's tax-exempt status, as you lead your congregation into the God-given duties of citizenship. Remember, as Edmund Burke warned, 'All that is necessary for the triumph of evil is for good men to do nothing'."[41]

The Christian Coalition's list of permissible political actions by churches provides an actual guide to the methods ministers can use to influence their congregations. The Christian Coalition provides ministers with the following instructions:

What Churches May Do

Conduct non-partisan voter registration drives.

Distribute non-partisan voter education materials, such as Christian Coalition voter guides and scorecards.

Host candidate or issue forums where all viable candidates are invited and allowed to speak.

Allow candidates and elected officials to speak at church services; if one is allowed to speak, others should not be prohibited from speaking.

Educate members about pending legislation.

Lobby for legislation and may spend no more than an insubstantial amount of its budget (five percent is safe) on direct lobbying activities.

Endorse candidates in their capacity as private citizens—A pastor does not lose his right to free speech because he is an employee of a church.

Participate fully in political committees that are independent of the church.

The Christian Coalition also provides boundaries for the political action of churches:

What Churches May Not Do

Endorse candidates directly or indirectly from the pulpit on behalf of the church.

Contribute funds or services (such as mailing lists or office equipment) directly to candidates or political committees.

Distribute materials that clearly favor any one candidate or political party.

Pay fees for partisan political events from church funds.

Allow candidates to solicit funds while speaking in church.

Set up a political committee that would contribute funds to political candidates.

The combination of the actual organization of the Christian Coalition and the political activity of ministers makes this a powerful organization. It certainly has helped to make pro-family and educational issues a central part of the Republican agenda. In 2004, the Christian Coalition stated as its goals:

- Strengthening the family.
- Protecting innocent human life.
- Returning education to local and parental control.
- Easing the tax burden on families.
- Punishing criminals and defending victims' rights.
- Protecting young people and our communities from the pollution of pornography.
- Defending the institution of marriage.
- Protecting religious freedom.[42]

EVOLUTION VERSUS CREATIONISM

The 2001 decision of the Kansas State Board of Education to reinstate the theory of evolution in the state's science curriculum was another episode in the ongoing struggle by the religiously oriented compassionate conservatives against evolutionary theory. For Christian fundamentalists, evolutionary theory contradicts the Word of God as literally interpreted from the Bible regarding the creation of humans. So-called "creationists" say a divine being created humans and other species. They say that because evolution cannot be observed or replicated in a laboratory, there is no evidence that it actually occurred. In the Kansas controversy the "big bang" theory, which contends that the universe was born from a vast explosion, had also been dropped from the curriculum.

The Kansas controversy echoed the famous 1920s Scopes trial, in which high school biology teacher John T. Scopes was accused of violating Tennessee's Butler Act, which forbade the teaching of evolutionary theory. Scopes was convicted of violating the law, but the verdict was later reversed on technical grounds by the state supreme court. However, the Butler Act remained in effect until 1967. Other states also have recently been embroiled in the evolution controversy. In Alabama, New Mexico, and Nebraska laws and administrative actions require that evolution be presented as theory that is merely one possible explanation. The Texas, Ohio, Washington, New Hampshire, and Tennessee legislatures defeated similar bills, including the requirement that teachers also present evidence to disprove the theory. Alabama now requires that biology textbooks contain a sticker calling evolution "a controversial theory some scientists present as a scientific explanation for the origin of living things." The sticker also warns the student that "No one was present when life first appeared on earth. Therefore, any statement about life's origins should be considered as theory, not fact."[43]

To members of the religiously oriented compassionate conservatives evolutionary theory is more than just a scientific dispute—it goes to the heart of the debate about values. Mark Looy of Answers in Genesis, a religious-right creationist group, said that "Students in public schools are being taught that evolution is a fact, that they're just products of survival of the fittest. There's not meaning in life if we're just animals in a struggle for survival. It creates a sense of purposelessness and hopelessness, which I think leads to things like pain, murder and suicide."[44]

The recent Kansas controversy over teaching evolutionary theory began in 1999, when the Kansas State Board of Education deleted it from the state's science curriculum. Although the action did not forbid schools from teaching the subject, it did remove the topic from the state's science tests. This meant that schools could ignore the theory while teaching biology without any resulting harm to students required to take the state's examinations. The issue originally arose in 1998, when the state board appointed a group of scientists to develop state standards for teaching science. When the standards were reviewed by the board, Steve Abrams, a conservative member of the board and former chairman of the state Republican party, declared it was "not good science to teach evolution as fact."[45] With the help of other religious fundamentalists, he rewrote the standards by deleting two pages on evolution while retaining a section on "micro-evolution" that dealt with genetic changes and natural selection within a species. In addition, Abrams added to the state standards "The design and complexity of the design of the cosmos requires [sic] an intelligent designer."[46] After much debate, the board adopted the rewritten standards by a vote of 6 to 4.

The decision of the Kansas State Board of Education created a political firestorm. Kansas Governor Bill Graves declared the new science standards "terrible" and "tragic," resulting in a split in the state's Republican party, with Gov. Graves supporting the moderate Republicans who favored the teaching of evolution and Kansas Sen. Sam Brownback supporting conservatives who opposed it.[47] The political controversy spilled over into the 2000 primary elections for the state board.

The 2000 primary election for the state board focused on the issue of evolution. Five of the 10 state board seats were to be voted on in the election following the primary. Because at the time Kansas was primarily a Republican state, primary outcomes often determine the final election. Voters, most of whom usually ignore the primary, paid close attention, with some actually switching from the Democratic to Republican parties so that they could vote for moderate Republicans. For instance, Democrat Lois Culver of suburban Kansas City denounced the science standards as an effort to put religion in the schools and declared, "I think this election is so critical to Kansas children that I was compelled to suck it up and change parties."[48] Culver announced her intention to vote for Sue Gamble, a moderate Republican who opposed the board's vote.

Groups outside of Kansas became embroiled in the political dispute. People for the American Way, a group organized for the specific purpose of countering the political actions of the religiously oriented compassionate conservatives, brought actor Ed Asner to the University of Kansas to re-enact the Scopes trial. Phillip Johnson, a University of California law professor, donated money to conservative candidates who espoused his belief in the "intelligent design" theory.[49]

During the primary election, moderate Republican Greg Musil ran television ads referring to the evolution controversy with the statement, "I'm embarrassed that Kansas is now being called a backward state."[50] Linda Holloway, the incumbent conservative Republican candidate, stated that she believed that evolution had been overemphasized in science teaching. Gamble, Holloway's moderate Republican opponent, declared that the science standards "put students at a disadvantage on a national level. You need to know about dinosaurs, the age of the earth."[51] Mary Douglass Brown, another conservative Republican candidate, warned, "There's a lot of money in evolution. To me, it's pseudoscience."[52]

Conservative candidates were defeated in the election. On February 14, 2001, the Kansas State Board of Education reversed its previous decision on evolution by a vote of 7 to 3. However, to placate conservative Christians, the board added to the science standards a statement: "'Understand' does not mandate 'belief.'"[53] In addition, the document instructed teachers that "While students may be required to understand some concepts that researchers use to conduct research and solve practical problems, they may accept or reject the scientific concepts presented. This applies particularly where students' and/or parents' beliefs may be at odds with the current scientific theories or concepts."[54]

Highlighting the political battles over ideas taught in schools, a warning to teachers was placed in the Kansas science standards that

> Teachers should not ridicule, belittle or embarrass a student for expressing an alternative view or belief. If a student should raise a question in a natural science class that the teacher determines to be outside the domain of science, the teacher should treat the question with respect. The teacher should explain

why the question is outside the domain of natural science and encourage the student to discuss the question further with his or her family and other appropriate sources.[55]

The evolutionary controversy in Kansas reflects one aspect of the continuing struggle by the religiously oriented compassionate conservatives to ensure conformity by public schools to their values. Of course, these actions must be placed in the context of other groups pounding on the school door demanding entry for their ideas and values. The difference in this case might be the size and organization of the religiously oriented compassionate conservatives as compared to other groups.

THE ORIGINS OF THE SCHOOL PRAYER SECTION OF NO CHILD LEFT BEHIND

As I discuss in this section, the school prayer section of No Child Left Behind (as noted in Item 6 of the legislative summary given on p. 3) emphasizes religious freedom in school in contrast to demands for a school prayer amendment to the U.S. Constitution. This resulted from a compromise reached after years of struggle over the U.S. Supreme Court's school prayer decision and the teaching of secular humanism in public schools. No Child Left Behind requires:

> The Secretary [U.S. Secretary of Education] shall provide and revise guidance, not later than September 1, 2002, and of every second year thereafter, to State educational agencies, local educational agencies, and the public on *constitutionally protected prayer* in public elementary schools and secondary schools, including making the guidance available on the Internet.[56]

Religion has always been a contentious issue in public schools. But recent efforts to focus on religious freedom in schools or what is called "constitutionally protected prayer" can be traced back to complaints about public schools teaching secular humanism. An important court case involving secular humanism began in 1983 in the schools of Hawkins County, Tennessee, when a local parent expressed concern about a new series of readers published by Holt, Rinehart & Winston. According to the complaint, the books were filled with "minorities, foreigners, environmentalism, women in nontraditional roles, and open-ended value judgments without clear right and wrong answers."[57]

The case attracted the attention of a wide variety of religious groups opposed to the teaching of secular humanism, such as Phyllis Schlafly's Eagle Forum, the National Association of Christian Educators, Citizens for Excellence in Education, Concerned Women for America, Pat Robertson's National Legal Foundation, and the American Family Association. In opposition to these groups was the liberal organization People for the American Way.

Criticism of the textbooks included a wide range of topics under the banner of secular humanism. Believing that unregulated capitalism was God's will, critics objected to suggestions of environmentalism because it led to government intervention in the economy. Protestors objected to teaching religious tolerance because it suggested that other religions were equal in value to Christianity. The teaching of international cooperation, evangelicals argued, could lead to world government, which would mean the reign of the antichrist. They also objected to stories that suggested humane treatment of animals and vegetarianism because God created animals for human use and exploitation. Evangelicals particularly objected to any story suggesting that hunting was wrong. Also, they felt that stories suggesting the depletion of resources and the extinction of species were denying God's promise to meet all human needs. Men and women portrayed in nontraditional roles would, according to protestors, destroy the traditional Christian family in which wives remained at home raising their children. For this reason, they opposed anything that smacked of feminism.[58]

After 4 years of litigation, the Sixth Circuit Court of Appeals ruled that public schools did not have to accommodate religious objections to the Holt, Rinehart & Winston readers. A previous lower court ruling suggested that religious objections to the books could be accommodated by assigning different texts or by teaching reading at home. The final ruling enhanced the power of school boards by requiring children attending public schools to read the books selected by school officials.[59]

In 1987, the National Legal Foundation, affiliated with Pat Robertson's Christian Broadcasting Network, provided support for an Alabama case against public schools teaching secular humanism. Robertson used his television show, *The 700 Club*, to publicize the case as a Christian battle against the antireligious tenets of secular humanism. People for the American Way and the American Civil Liberties Union provided legal opposition to the work of the National Legal Foundation. The case received a great deal of attention when Robertson announced his candidacy for the Presidency in 1988.[60]

The plaintiffs charged that 45 textbooks approved for Alabama schools taught secular humanism. Supporting their case was a consent decree signed by Alabama's Gov. George Wallace stating that the religion of secular humanism should be excluded from Alabama schools. On *The 700 Club*, Robertson quoted Gov. Wallace, who said, "I don't want to teach ungodly humanism in the schools where I'm governor." In turn, Robertson declared that taking secular humanism out of the schools was an issue of "religious freedom."[61]

The primary legal problem for the plaintiffs was proving that secular humanism was a religion. Again, the issue was about textbooks teaching children that they could make their own moral decisions without relying on the authority of the Word of God. In a lower court decision, religious conservative Judge Brevard Hand ruled that secular humanism was indeed a religion and that the use of books espousing secular humanism should be removed from the schools. This decision was reversed by the Eleventh Circuit Court of Appeals, which ruled that the books did not violate the First Amendment: "Rather the message conveyed is one of a governmental attempt to instill in Alabama public school children such values as independent thought, tolerance of diverse views, self-respect, maturity, self-reliance, and logical decision-making. This is an entirely appropriate secular effect."[62]

The Christian Coalition later adopted Robertson's claim that secular humanism, along with school prayer, was an issue of religious freedom. Beginning in the 1980 Presidential election, the Republican Party supported the idea of a constitutional amendment allowing school prayers. Reflecting what was now becoming a historic position for the Republican Party, Haley Barbour, Chairman of the National Republican Committee, stated in 1996 that the Republican Party supported the "right to voluntary prayer in schools ... whether through a constitutional amendment or through legislation, or a combination of both."[63]

In 1994, after failing to achieve a school prayer amendment, the Christian Coalition decided to make what Reed called a "seismic shift" in strategy. Rather than campaigning for school prayer, the decision was made to adopt Robertson's language and support an amendment for religious freedom. Reed argued that an emphasis on religious freedom as opposed to the narrower issue of school prayer would appeal to a broader religious audience. The religious freedom amendment would guarantee the right of religious expression to all people in all public settings.[64]

In addition, the Christian Coalition believes that a religious-freedom amendment would protect the rights of students to express their religious beliefs in the classroom. For instance, a student would have the right to support creationism over evolutionary theory in science classes. In supporting the religious-freedom amendment, Reed described the case of a Tennessee high school student, Brittney Settle, who was failed for turning in an essay on the life of Jesus Christ. Without citing the details of the case, Reed claimed that a federal court upheld the right of the school to flunk the student for her religious beliefs. In reaction to the case, Reed stated, "A religious freedom amendment would protect her, along with unbelieving students who are nervous about being compelled to participate in mandatory religious exercises in public schools."[65]

Reps. Newt Gingrich and Dick Armey promised the Christian Coalition that for its support of Republican candidates they would introduce a proposal for inclusion of religious freedom in the First Amendment. When the House Judiciary Committee held hearings in July 1996 on the proposed changes, members of Americans United for Separation of Church and State and other religious groups held a protest in front of the Supreme Court. The proposed changes to the First Amendment would "protect religious freedom, including the right of students in public schools to pray without government sponsorship or compulsion." In addition, the changes would prohibit state and federal governments from denying anyone "equal access to a benefit, or otherwise discriminate against any person, on account of religious belief, expression, or exercise."[66]

During the hearings, the head of the Judiciary Committee, Republican Rep. Henry Hyde, complained that public school teachers often discriminated against Christians by denying reports and essays on Jesus Christ. "Public school teachers, who accept reports on witches," Hyde explained, "forbid students from writing reports on Jesus. This is madness."[67] One cynical critic, David Ramage, Jr., president emeritus of the McCormick Theological Seminary, accused the Christian Coalition of wanting to rush the amendments through the House of Representatives so that House members' positions could be included in their fall voting guide. Voting "no" on the religious-freedom changes, Ramage suggested, would be listed in the Christian Coalition's voter guide as "a vote against religious freedom" or a "vote against God."[68]

The school prayer section of No Child Left Behind mandates the protection of religious freedom in public schools. The legislation requires the U.S. Secretary of Education to issue guidance for protecting constitutionally approved prayer. Dated February 7, 2003, the U.S. Department of Education guide reminds local education agencies that they must report that their schools have "no policy that prevents, or otherwise denies participation in, constitutionally protected prayer in public schools as set forth in this guidance."[69] The guidelines state,

> Although the Constitution forbids public school officials from directing or favoring prayer, students do not "shed their constitutional rights to freedom of speech or expression at the schoolhouse gate," and the Supreme Court has made clear that "private religious speech, far from being a First Amendment orphan, is as fully protected under the Free Speech Clause as secular private expression." Moreover, not all religious speech that takes place in the public schools or at school-sponsored events is governmental speech. For example, "nothing in the Constitution … prohibits any public school student from voluntarily praying at any time before, during, or after the school day," and students may pray with fellow students during the school day on the same terms and conditions that they may engage in other conversation or speech. Likewise, local school authorities possess substantial discretion to impose rules of order and pedagogical restrictions on student activities, but they may not

structure or administer such rules to discriminate against student prayer or religious speech.[70]

SEX EDUCATION AND PORNOGRAPHY

Concerns about sex education and pornography appear in the 2004 Republican Platform and No Child Left Behind. Personal sexual values are a central concern for religiously oriented compassionate conservatives who believe that personal values determine the success or failure of societies and democratic governments. Also, among some religious groups, thinking and imagining sexual activities is the same as engaging in them. Consequently, compassionate conservatives believe that control of pornography and sex education programs that teach abstinence from sexual activity are essential for building character traits that value hard work, personal advancement, and a democratic society. And, of course, sexual abstinence reduces the spread of sexually transmitted disease. Compassionate conservatives believe that teaching about the use of condoms and other preventive devices against transmission of sexual diseases only encourages sexual activity. While the use of condoms might reduce the transmission of sexual diseases, compassionate conservatives argue, it opens the door to teenage sexual promiscuity which undermines the values of a democratic society.

The concern with sexuality is based on the principle that ideas, as opposed to material conditions, determine the course of civilization. Reflecting on his experience as a student in a Roman Catholic high school where the Jesuit teachers made the possession of pornography a reason for expulsion, Pat Buchanan explains: "Far greater harm has come, not only to souls but to nations, from polluted books and evil ideas—racism, militarism, Nazism, Communism—than has ever come from polluted streams or rotten food. With the Bible [the Jesuit teachers] taught that it is not what goes in the stomach that "defiles a man, but what comes out of his mouth."[71]

Concerns about sexual values are explicitly addressed in the 2004 Republican Platform which advocates abstinence education:

> We support efforts to educate teens and parents about the health risks associated with early sexual activity and provide the tools needed to help teens make healthy choices. Abstinence from sexual activity is the only protection that is 100 percent effective against out-of-wedlock pregnancies and sexually transmitted diseases, including sexually transmitted HIV/AIDS. Therefore, we support doubling abstinence education funding.[72]

Also, No Child Left Behind explicitly prohibits the distribution of federal funds to schools that "provide sex education or HIV prevention education in schools unless that instruction is age appropriate and includes the health benefits of abstinence." Also, schools are prohibited from operating "a program of contraceptive distribution"[73]

The 2004 Republican Platform criticizes the use of the First Amendment to the U.S. Constitution to protect pornography and accepts a U.S. Supreme Court ruling that "to equate the free and robust exchange of ideas and political debate with commercial exploitation of obscene material demeans the grand conception of the first amendment and its high purposes in the historic struggle for freedom."[74] Also, the Republican Platform states, "With ever more children accessing material over the Internet, we support efforts to bolster online protections that prevent children from being exposed to pornographic images and solicitations."[75] Under No Child Left Behind's "Title II—Preparing, Training and Recruiting High Quality Teachers and Principals," schools must have in place "a policy of Internet safety for minors … that protects against access through such computers to visual depictions that are (i) obscene; (ii) child pornography; or (iii) harmful to minors."[76]

In addition, religiously oriented compassionate conservatives believe that homosexuality destroys the moral fabric of a democracy. The 2004 Republican Platform calls for a Constitutional Amendment that would make gay/lesbian marriages legal: "We strongly support President Bush's call for a Constitutional amendment that fully protects marriage …. We believe, and social science confirms, that the well-being of children is best accomplished in the environment of the home, nurtured by their mother and father anchored by the bonds of marriage."[77] Historically, evangelical groups have pressured Republican administrations to distribute only abstinence-oriented sex education programs. In 1991, for example, the American Civil Liberties Union objected to federal sponsorship of Teen Choice and other groups advocating chastity as the solution to teenage pregnancy, claiming that federally sponsored material was filled with religious references that violated the First Amendment. The material advised teenagers to "pray together and invite God on every date." The ACLU also objected to the statement "God is supreme … God does exist."[78]

Acceptance of discrimination against gays and lesbians is explicit in the No Child Left Behind's Boy Scouts of America Equal Access Act (as noted in Item 5 of the legislative summary given previously). In the 1990s, the decision by the Boy Scouts of America to deny membership to homosexuals was extremely contentious. In 2000, the U.S. Supreme Court ruled in *Boy Scouts of America v. Dale* that the Boy Scouts was a private association and had the right to set its own standards for membership and leadership. As a result, school districts across the country banned the Boy Scouts from using school facilities because they discriminated against homosexuals. In the Boy Scouts of America Equal Access Act of No Child Left Behind, public schools receiving funds under the legislation are prohibited from denying Boy Scouts use of school facilities. The legislation states, "Notwithstanding any other provision of law, no public elementary school, public secondary school, local educational agency, or State educational agency that has a designated open forum or a limited public forum and that receives funds made available through the Department shall deny equal access or a fair opportunity to meet to, or discriminate against, any group officially affiliated with the Boy Scouts of America."[79]

The religiously oriented compassionate conservatives condemn any instruction or positive statements about homosexuality. For the Christian Coalition and other members of the religiously oriented compassionate conservatives, homosexuality should be publicly condemned. Buchanan argued that gay men should be blamed for bringing about the AIDS plague. In fact, the Christian Coalition's first membership drive in 1989 focused on the National Endowment for the Arts sponsorship of the homoerotic photographs of Robert Mapplethorpe.[80]

In 1995, the Christian Coalition placed strong political pressure on Congress to censure pornography on the World Wide Web and television. In its effort to remove pornography or, as it is called, cyberporn, from the World Wide Web, the Christian Coalition sought the aid of Democrats after Massachusetts Democratic Rep. Edward Markey introduced a bill requiring television manufacturers to install "v-chips" to allow parents to block programs with too much violence.[81]

Working with a group of Democrats and Republicans, the Christian Coalition claimed a major responsibility for the writing of the 1995 Telecommunications Act requiring censorship of cyberporn and v-chips. Reed believes that passage of the telecommunications legislation moved the Christian Coalition from simple criticism of legislative action to the exercise of legislative power. Reed and other coalition members sat down with members of Congress and worked out the details of the telecommunications legislation.

The work on the telecommunications bill demonstrated that the Christian Coalition could influence both political parties. Reed argues that the relationship between evangelical Christians and the Republican Party is simply strategic. "The two are not one and the same," he stated. "Indeed, the partnership between the profamily movement and the GOP is less a romance than a shotgun wedding."[82]

MULTICULTURAL EDUCATION

Another major area of concern for the religiously oriented compassionate conservatives is multicultural curricula. Implicitly, No Child Left Behind's English Language Acquisition, Language Enhancement, and Academic Achievement Act rejects cultural pluralism by replacing the Office of Bilingual Education, which was established by the 1968 Bilingual Education Act. The purpose of the 1968 Bilingual Education Act was to protect the cultures and languages of conquered peoples. The Bilingual Education Act was the result of the political activities of Native Americans, Puerto Ricans, and Mexican Americans. All three groups considered themselves victims of U.S. imperialism. In the 19th century, the U.S. government carried out a policy of conquering of Native American lands and of trying to eradicate Native American languages and cultures. The Mexican American War resulted in the U.S. government permanently occupying the northern half of Mexico, including Texas, California, Arizona, New Mexico, Nevada, and Colorado. School policies in these areas also attempted to eradicate the culture and language of the conquered Mexican population. Puerto Rico was conquered by the United States during the 1898 Spanish-American War and there was also an attempt to eradicate local languages and cultures. Therefore, it is important to note that bilingual education received its political support from groups wanting to maintain their cultures and languages, and envisioned a pluralistic or multicultural American society.[83]

Evangelical Christians do not believe, as mentioned before, in teaching tolerance of other religions including Native American religions. For evangelicals, Christianity is the only true religion. In addition, the religiously oriented compassionate conservatives believe that the Judeo-Christian foundation of American culture makes it superior to other cultures. Therefore, instruction should emphasize the inculcation of Judeo-Christian culture and not tolerance for other cultures.

In 1986, William Bennett made a name for himself in academic circles when he launched a public attack against the Stanford University faculty for replacing a freshman undergraduate course entitled "Western Culture," in which students read 15 works in Western philosophy and literature, with a course entitled "Cultures, Ideas, and Values," in which readings would include works by "women, minorities, and persons of color."[84] Bennett argued that students should be required to study Western culture because it provides the framework for American government and culture. In addition, he stated, "Probably most difficult for the critics of Western culture to acknowledge is that 'the West is good.'" Western culture, according to Bennett, has "set the moral, political, economic, and social standards for the rest of the world."[85]

In 1994, issues of religion, sex, and multiculturalism came together in a bitter struggle among the governor of California, the state legislature, and educators over a proposed statewide test for grades K–12. The storm over the test, originally called the California Learning Assessment System test and later the California Comprehensive Assessment System, erupted when author Alice Walker and the People for the American Way objected to state education officials removing from the test two of Walker's stories.

One story, "Roselily," was removed because of objections by the Traditional Values Coalition, a religiously oriented compassionate conservatives organization. The story dealt with a Christian woman in rural Mississippi marrying a Muslim, and it was considered antireligious. Beverly Sheldon, research director for the Traditional Values Coalition, argued that the test would influence the religious values of students. The other story by Walker was removed because a member of the state board of education considered it hostile to meat eating. As mentioned previously in the discussion of the Tennessee case, evangelicals believe God put animals on earth to be eaten and exploited by humans. The People for the American Way objected to the removal of the stories because it sent "a chilling message across the country of the threat to educational freedom and constitutional rights posed by extremist pressure groups."[86]

By May of 1994, hundreds of people were turning out for school board meetings throughout California to support or protest the test. Some of the protests were about a rumored question depicting a barber contemplating the slitting of a customer's throat. A Los Angeles school board member, Sue Stokka, objected on the basis that the test did not emphasize basic skills. A temporary restraining order against giving the test in the San Bernadino school district was issued by a superior court judge after a suit was filed by the conservative Rutherford Institute. The school board in the Antelope Valley Union High School district voted not to give the test.

By September of 1994 the test was a major political issue. Gov. Pete Wilson, who was running for re-election in November, threatened to veto a reauthorization of the testing program. A new objection to the test program was raised when a study found that men, Latinos, and Asian Americans were underrepresented among the groups that developed the test questions. A new legislative bill called for the exclusion of all questions related to personal beliefs regarding family life, gender, and religion.[87]

The religiously oriented compassionate conservatives' stance against multiculturalism is reflected in the 1996 Republican platform's call for an emphasis in schools on teaching about Western civilization and its pledge to make English the official language of the United States. The platform vowed to create an education consumer's warranty which, among other things, would guarantee that all American children would "learn the nation's history and democratic values and study the classics of Western civilization."[88] In addition, the platform proposed that "To reinforce our American heritage … [states and local school boards require] our public schools to dedicate one full day each year solely to studying the Declaration of Independence and the Constitution."[89] With regard to the language issue, the platform clearly stated: "We support the official recognition of English as the nation's common language."[90]

LIBERAL DOMINATION OF EDUCATION AND CULTURE

There is a strong populist rhetoric running through the statements of the religiously oriented compassionate conservatives. Even New Democrats claim that they want to reduce the power of the federal government and return the control of public institutions to the people. Arguments for school choice emphasize breaking the stranglehold of an educational bureaucracy and returning power over schooling to parents. A great deal of the rhetoric is antigovernment and is filled with complaints that government agencies and bureaucrats represent a third class that, for its own benefit, has seized power from the people.

Many compassionate conservatives believe the liberal elite is composed of both cultural and government leaders. William Bennett argued that the cultural war is between the beliefs held by most citizens and "the beliefs of a liberal elite that today dominates many of our institutions and who therefore exert influence on American life and culture."[91] This liberal elite, according to Bennett, inhabits universities, the literary and artistic worlds, liberal religious institutions, and the media. The liberal elite, according to Bennett, is different from former bourgeois elites, who valued the importance of the family, public morality, hard work, and individual entrepreneurship. In contrast, the liberal elite rejects many traditional Christian values and looks with scorn on Americans who believe in the value of hard work and economic individualism. Furthermore, this liberal elite supports ideas that are anathema to the religiously oriented compassionate conservatives, such as multiculturalism, sexual freedom, and gay and lesbian relationships.

From the perspective of the religiously oriented compassionate conservatives, it is the combination of government bureaucrats and the liberal elite that is responsible for imposing unwanted government policies and values on the public. For instance, southern Whites and northern ethnic Whites—the important new constituencies in the Republican Party—showed open resentment for school desegregation, particularly for the method of forced busing. From their viewpoint, desegregation policies were forced on them by a liberal Supreme Court and liberal educational bureaucrats and were supported by liberal elites living in suburbs protected from the effects of integration.

For religious fundamentalists, it was a combination of a liberal Supreme Court and liberal government bureaucrats that replaced prayers and Bible reading in public schools with secular humanism. As the religious fundamentalists see it, a combination of liberal writers and educational bureaucrats have forced textbooks on schools that undercut evangelical values. From this perspective, it is the influence of liberal cultural elites that results in textbooks containing the values of vegetarianism, one-worldism, and secular humanism. It is liberal elites who promote sex education programs filled with teaching about birth control, homosexuality, and AIDS. It is liberal elites who are responsible for the sexuality and violence in movies and television programs that, from the perspective of the religiously oriented compassionate conservatives, undermine family values and increase crime rates.

It is important to understand that the resentment against the so-called liberal elite and government bureaucrats is based on real policies that were, in fact, imposed on many unwilling citizens. This does not mean that these policies were wrong but that they were not initiated by the communities most affected by them. In reality, there do exist government officials, legal experts, and media elites who do not represent the values of the religiously oriented compassionate conservatives and segregationists. Therefore, the opposition to educational and government bureaucrats and the desire to return power to the people is based on the assumption that this will restore traditional values to education.

CONCLUSION

In summary, compassionate conservativism is embodied in the No Child Left Behind Act in sections dealing with character education, school prayer, censorship of pornography, bilingual education, abstinence education, and the Boy Scouts. Also, discussions of educational standards and testing can be considered as enhancing the self-help aspects of compassionate conservatism. If educational standards and testing increase the quality of schooling then they might provide graduates, particularly those from low-income families, with the tools by which they can lift themselves up the economic ladder. The assumption of compassionate conservativism is that personal values, particularly religious values, are necessary for maintaining a democratic society, and that poverty is primarily the result of failed personal character. Improving personal values and eliminating poverty, compassionate conservatives believe, can be accomplished in public schools through character training, protecting religious freedom, teaching abstinence from sexual activity until marriage, avoiding the maintenance of cultures other than "American" culture, by not condoning homosexuality, and by ensuring that all children learn.

Neoconservatism and No Child Left Behind: The Republican Educational Agenda for the 21st Century

Neoconservative educational reforms are embodied in the educational standards, testing, and choice sections (Items 1 and 3 of the legislative summary given in chapter 1) of the No Child Left Behind Act. Neoconservatives believe in the value of free markets in shaping public institutions, including public schools. Their ideal is free competition between public and private schools in attracting students. Supposedly, consumer (or in this case parental) choice would force schools to improve in order to attract customers. This model is similar to choosing breakfast cereal in a supermarket. Those breakfast cereals without buyers would be forced to discontinue or change.

While neoconservatives advocate a free market for schools, they retain the traditional conservative view that the government should regulate social behavior which, in this case, means the activities of public schools. The free market of schools, according to neoconservatives, should be regulated. The regulation of schools, neoconservatives argue, should be through the creation of state educational curriculum standards and the measurement of student progress by standardized tests. Also, public reports of student scores on standardized tests would provide parents with information by which they could make a rational choice in a marketplace of schools.

The neoconservative hope of a free market in public schools has been thwarted by a combination of public resistance to the idea and the constitutional requirement, in the case of private religious schools, of separation of religion and the state. However, the idea of school choice does find its way into No Child Left Behind in a modified form. The legislation requires that parents be offered the choice of other public schools if their children attend a school that fails to achieve adequate yearly progress 2 years in a row. Also, under Title V of No Child Left Behind, funds are allocated to promote "Informed Parental Choice."

In keeping with the neoconservative belief that the education marketplace should be regulated by state standards and testing, and that the consumer, can make informed judgments about schools, No Child Left Behind requires the dissemination of state and local report cards containing student achievement scores. Also, public reaction to report cards is suppose to create public pressure to improve failing schools. The legislation specifies that report cards are to be concise and understandable to parents. The specifications for the content of local report cards are:

(I) the number and percentage of schools identified for school improvement … and how long the schools have been so identified; and

(II) information that shows how students served by the local educational agency achieved on the statewide academic assessment compared to students in the State as a whole; and

(ii) in the case of a school—

(I) whether the school has been identified for school improvement; and

(II) information that shows how the school's students' achievement on the statewide academic assessments and other indicators of adequate yearly progress compared to students in the local educational agency and the State as a whole.[1]

FREE MARKETS AND SCHOOL CHOICE

Neoconservative ideas about free markets and school choice can be traced to the work of Friedrich Hayek, an Austrian economist and Nobel Prize winner, who moved to the United States to teach at the University of Chicago from 1950 to 1962. Hayek influenced a number of American economists, including Murray Rothbard, William Simon, and Milton Friedman. In their most radical anarcholibertarian form, Austrian economists such as Rothbard advocated abolishing all forms of government and applying free-market theory to every aspect of living, including highways, law enforcement, defense, and schooling.[2] Without government interference, these Austrian economists argued, marketplace competition would create ideal institutions. Applied to schooling, this meant no government provision or control of education. Instead, entrepreneurs would organize schools and compete for students while the "invisible hand" of the marketplace determined what forms of schooling were best.

Hayek's economic ideas played a major role in the Reagan-style Republicanism of the 1980s and 1990s and in conservative attacks on liberalism and government bureaucracy. In the 1930s, Hayek debated English economist

John Maynard Keynes over the role of government in a capitalist system. Keynes argued that for capitalism to survive governments needed to intervene in the economy. Classical liberals, such as John Stuart Mill, opposed government intervention, but the progressive liberals of the 1930s justified government intervention to ensure equality of opportunity and provide a social safety net as necessary for the survival of capitalism.[3]

In *The Road to Serfdom,* Hayek set the stage for later conservative criticisms of government bureaucracies, including educational bureaucracies. He argued that the difficulty of determining prices or the value of goods would inevitably cause the failure of centrally planned economies. According to Hayek, pricing determines the social value of goods: What should a car cost in relation to food? What should the price of health care be in relation to education? In a free market, Hayek asserted, prices or social values are determined by individual choice. In a planned economy, pricing or social value is determined by a government bureaucracy. What criterion is used by a government bureaucracy? Hayek's answer was that the inevitable criterion is one that promotes the personal advantage of bureaucracy members. In addition, bureaucrats and intellectuals supported by a bureaucracy will advance social theories that vindicate the continued existence and expansion of the bureaucracy.[4]

Defining the enemy as the bureaucracy is one of Hayek's enduring legacies. Many educational critics complain that the problem with public schools is the educational bureaucracy. A frequently heard statement regarding schools is: "The problem is not money! The problem is bureaucratic waste!" By placing the blame on the educational bureaucracy, school reformers can avoid the issue of equal funding among school districts. Some public school students receive the benefits of living in well-financed suburban school districts, whereas others languish in overcrowded classrooms in poorly funded school districts that lack adequate textbooks and educational materials. Blaming the bureaucracy became an easy method for avoiding increased educational funding.

Beginning in the 1950s and lasting into the 21st century, neoconservatives claimed that a major problem is control of schools by a self-serving educational bureaucracy. In addition, as discussed in chapter 1, right-wing Republicans insist that a liberal elite controls the culture of universities, public schools, and the media. Hayek identified this liberal elite as a new class composed of government experts and their intellectual supporters. Within this framework, schools could improve only if the power of the educational bureaucrats was broken and schools functioned according to the dictates of market competition.

Friedman, a colleague of Hayek's at the University of Chicago and 1976 Nobel Prize winner, became the first American, at least to my knowledge, to advocate the use of vouchers as a means of providing school choice. In contrast to Rothbard, Friedman argued that the benefits of maintaining a stable and democratic society justified government support of education, but not government-operated schools. Friedman proposed a government-financed voucher that parents could redeem "for a specified maximum sum per child per year if spent on 'approved' educational services."[5] Friedman believed the resulting competition between private schools for government vouchers would improve the quality of education.

With arguments similar to those heard in the 1990s that vouchers or tuition tax credits would improve the quality of education, Friedman contended in the 1960s that vouchers would overcome the class stratification that results from the existence of rich and poor school districts. As Friedman suggested, "Under present arrangements, stratification of residential areas effectively restricts the intermingling of children from decidedly different backgrounds."[6] Except for a few parochial schools, Friedman argued, private schools were too expensive for most families, which resulted in further social class divisions in education.

Like Friedman, many neoconservatives embraced the concept of the free market but rejected the idea of completely abandoning government control, particularly social and moral control. After the riots and student rebellions of the 1960s and 1970s, neoconservatives believed that the government should exercise moral authority over social life but, accepting the idea of the free market for business, they believed that the government should not interfere in the economy.

PLANNING AN EDUCATIONAL REVOLUTION: THE TRICKLE-DOWN THEORY OF IDEAS AND NO CHILD LEFT BEHIND

Selling the public on vouchers and free markets, and eventually academic standards and testing, was the result of conscious efforts by conservative private foundations to recruit scholars and disseminate their agendas for education. Their efforts paid off with passage of No Child Left Behind. My first realization of this attempt to revolutionize education occurred in the early 1970s, at a meeting at the Institute for Humane Studies in Menlo Park, California. Discussion at the meeting focused on how to organize a cadre of intellectuals to openly support freedom and capitalism because colleges and universities were hopelessly controlled by left-wing intellectuals. I was one of those academics, they hoped, who could be persuaded to spread conservative ideas into academic establishments and to policymakers. Being elitists, these conservatives wanted to focus their efforts on intellectual and political leaders. Just as supply-side economists would later talk about trickle-down economics, these conservatives believed in trickle-down ideas.

At the time, I did not understand this to be part of a movement later described by James Smith in his 1991 book *The Idea Brokers:* "In the early 1970s, executives in a handful of traditionally conservative foundations redefined their programs with the aim of shaping the public policy agenda and constructing a network of conservative institutions and scholars."[7] One of the leaders and articulate spokespersons of this movement was William Simon, who left his job in 1976 as Secretary of the Treasury in the Nixon and Ford administrations to become head of the John Olin Foundation, the purpose of which, in Simon's words, "is to support those individuals and institutions who are working to strengthen the free enterprise system."[8]

Reflecting Simon's economic beliefs, the preface and foreword for his book *A Time for Truth* were written, respectively, by Friedman and Hayek. In the preface, Friedman sounded the warning that intellectual life in the United States was under the control of "socialists and interventionists, who have wrongfully appropriated in this country the noble label 'liberal' and who have been the intellectual architects of our suicidal course."[9] Applying concepts of the marketplace to intellectual life, Friedman argued that the payoff for these "liberals" was support by an entrenched government bureaucracy. In other words, the liberal elite and the government bureaucracy fed off each other. Using a phrase that would be repeated by conservatives throughout the rest of the 20th century, Friedman contended that "the view that government is the problem, not the cure," is hard for the public to understand.[10] According to Friedman's plea, saving the country required a group of intellectuals to promote a general understanding of the importance of the free market.

To undermine the supposed rule of a liberal intelligentsia, Simon urged the business community to support intellectuals who advocate the importance of the free market. Simon called on businesspeople to stop supporting colleges and universities that produced "young collectivists by the thousands" and media "which serve as megaphones for anticapitalist opinion." In both cases, Simon insisted, businesspeople should focus their support on university programs and media that stress procapitalist ideas.[11]

In his call for action, Simon calculated that the first step should involve businesspeople rushing "multimillions to the aid of liberty, in the many places where it is beleaguered." On receiving the largesse of business, he insisted, "Foundations imbued with the philosophy of freedom ... must take pains to funnel desperately needed funds to scholars, social scientists, writers, and journalists who understand the relationship between political and economic liberty."[12] In light of Simon's remarks as head of the John Olin

Foundation in the 1970s, it is interesting that two of the leading writers for the conservative cause in education, Chester Finn, Jr. and Dinesh D'Souza, are, respectively, John Olin Fellow at the Manhattan Institute and the American Enterprise Institute. Besides supporting scholars at the conservative Manhattan Institute and the American Enterprise Institute, the John Olin Foundation, with assets of $90 million, backed many right-wing causes and, according to one writer, "its pattern of giving became [in the 1970s] more sophisticated and more closely attuned to the potential of grantees for influencing debates on national politics."[13]

Although conservatives talk about the invisible hand of the free market, the trickle-down distribution of ideas has been very well planned, with the following methods being used:

1. Creating foundations and institutes that fund research and policy statements supportive of school choice, privatization of public schools and, more recently, charter schools.
2. Identifying scholars to conduct research, write policy statements, and lecture at public forums that are favorable to school choice, privatization of public schools, and charter schools.
3. Financing conferences to bring like-minded scholars together for the sharing of ideas and the creation of edited books.
4. Paying scholars to write newspaper opinion pieces that are then distributed to hundreds of newspapers across the country.

This fourth point is an important element in the trickle-down theory of ideas. It is a big leap from writing a research report to being featured on the opinion-editorial page of the *New York Times* or other leading newspapers. This frequently occurs with conservatively backed educational commentators, such as Chester Finn, Jr. and Diane Ravitch. It requires connections and a public relations staff to gain quick access to the media. Providing this type of access is one of the important elements in the strategy of spreading the conservative agenda. With public relations help from conservatives, I appeared in the 1970s as an "academic expert" on radio and television shows across the country. On one occasion, after the exercise portion of an early morning television show, I fielded call-in questions ranging from "Why can't my daughter read?" to "Why are all college professors socialists?" There was never any hint that my appearance on the program resulted from the work of conservative organizations.

In *The Transformation of American Politics: The New Washington and the Rise of Think Tanks,* David Ricci described the attempt to mobilize and control public opinion. "Those who talked about developing conservative ideas," Ricci stated, "were committed not just to producing them but to the commercial concept of a product, in the sense of something that, once created, must be placed before the public as effectively as possible."[14]

THE MANHATTAN INSTITUTE
AND GEORGE W. BUSH'S PRESIDENCY

An important foundation that markets neoconservative ideas is the Manhattan Institute. In the 1990s, the Manhattan Institute funded reactionary scholars such as Richard J. Hernstein and Charles Murray to write *The Bell Curve: Intelligence and Class Structure in American Life*. And in 2001, President George W. Bush entered the White House with the backing of the Manhattan Institute and favoring its educational policies.

Under the banner "Turning Intellect Into Influence," the Manhattan Institute's Web site proudly lists its influence on Bush's administration. First on the list are two carriers of the torch of conservative compassionism as preached by Marvin Olasky and supported by the institute. The Manhattan Institute's John Dilulio was appointed Director of the White House Office of Faith-Based and Community Initiatives, and Stephen Goldsmith was named Special Advisor to the President for Faith-Based and Community Initiatives. Influence on economic policy was ensured by the institute's former Senior Fellow Lawrence Lindsay acting as Chief Economic Advisor to Bush and the appointment of the Institute's David Frum as Special Assistant to the President for Economic Speech Writing. While at the Institute, Lindsay wrote the book that influenced Bush's tax policies: *The Growth Experiment: How the New Tax Policy Is Transforming the U.S. Economy*. The institute's influence on civil rights issues was assured by the appointment of Senior Fellow Abigail Thernstrom to the U.S. Commission on Civil Rights. Also, of course, the institute cited Senior Fellow Myron Magnet's book, *The Dream and the Nightmare* ... [as] 'The book that helped shape Bush's message.'"[15]

The Manhattan Institute devotes a great of attention to school choice and testing. At the Center for Civic Innovation of the Manhattan Institute, Jay Greene works as Senior Fellow in the field of education and heads the Manhattan Institute's Florida-based Education Research Office. According to the 2004 Manhattan Institute's Web site, Jay Greene's work

> on education reform focuses on improving two main reforms of public education: school choice and accountability. School choice reforms (including charter schools and school vouchers) are dedicated to improving the options available to parents of children in public schools, and making public schools more directly accountable to parents for education outcomes. Accountability reforms are devoted to improving educational achievement by focusing on imparting knowledge and skills and making teachers, administrators, and students accountable for success or failure.[16]

The Manhattan Institute's influence on national educational policies involves an amalgamation of politics and think tank intellectuals. The Manhattan Institute is a nonprofit organization that funds scholarly work for the purpose of influencing public policy. "The Manhattan Institute," the opening line posted on its Web site declares, "has been an important force in shaping American political culture."[17] This is followed by the statement "We have supported and publicized research on our era's most challenging public policy issues: taxes, welfare, crime, the legal system, urban life, race, education, and many other topics."[18]

Even more revealing of its open use of scholarship to promote certain political and educational causes is the statement accompanying its plea for donations. Written by the institute's trustee, Walter Wriston, the contribution form contends that "The Institute's intellectual capital far exceeds its financial capital, making it the most cost-effective organization of its kind. Although the impact of our ideas dwarfs our financial resources, we still need the latter. There is not a better bargain to be had."[19] At the bottom of the form the contributor is asked if he or she wants to receive e-mail updates on "Education Reform," "Welfare Reform," "Crime Reduction," "Faith-Based Initiatives," "Race and Ethnicity Initiatives," and "Legal Reform."[20]

Educational policy was Bush's topic when he spoke at the Manhattan Institute during the 2000 primary campaign. At the institute, Bush was warmly greeted as "my homeboy" by former congressman Rev. Floyd Flake.[21] In this tangled web of connections, Flake had, just before introducing Bush, accepted the headship of the charter school division of the Edison Schools Inc., the largest for-profit school-management company in the country. Flake is listed on the "Education Reform" section of the institute's Web site, along with former U.S. Department of Education Assistant Secretaries Chester E. Finn, Jr., and Diane Ravitch, as being "at the forefront of today's thinking about how our children's educational achievement can be increased."[22] Finn is identified on the Web site as the John M. Olin Fellow at the institute. I have more to say about Finn, Ravitch, and the Olin Foundation later in this chapter.

Bush's proposal to give vouchers to parents of children in failing schools closely parallels the policies promoted by the Manhattan Institute, which has close links to William Simon's John Olin Foundation. During the 2000 campaign, the Republican Party platform advocated the empowerment of "needy families to escape persistently failing schools by allowing federal dollars to follow their children to the school of their choice."[23] Bush and Republican leaders contemplated that parents whose children were in schools that consistently had failing test scores would be given the choice of using federal Title I funds to send their children to private schools. This plan would eventually become part of No Child Left Behind. It was similar to the one praised in the Manhattan Institute's publication on Florida's A-Plus accountability and school choice program, operated under the leadership of George W. Bush's brother, Gov. Jeb Bush. The institute's report, authored by Jay P. Greene, claimed that "By offering vouchers to students at failing schools, the Florida A-Plus choice and accountability system was intended to motivate those schools to improve …. This report found that students' academic test scores improve when public schools are faced with the prospect that their students will receive vouchers."[24]

At a 1999 luncheon at the Manhattan Institute, Jeb Bush described what he called the "Bush/Brogan A+ Plan for Education" in the following words: "In Florida today, every school is graded on an A through F scale. We said that when a school has been rated F for two out of four years, that school would be defined as a failure, and the parents in those schools would be given other options." One of the options Bush described were scholarships that "would enable [parents] to choose a private school for their child, religious or non-religious, so long as the private school admitted all applicants, accepted the opportunity scholarship amount as full tuition, and used the same standardized tests as used by our public schools."[25]

Vouchers are a target area on the Manhattan Institute's educational agenda. With the objective of influencing public debate, the institute's official program description states that "Educational reform is the top public policy concern today, so it should come as no surprise that the Manhattan Institute has the best education reform experts in the country to offer practical advice to policymakers."[26] Also, as part of its research agenda, the institute is focusing on vouchers as a method for helping low-income parents escape public schools.

The institute's research on vouchers is not a search for truth but a search for justifications for its political program. An objective research program would seek to find out if vouchers are an effective means of improving school conditions. However, the institute's program statements indicate a belief that vouchers are the solution: "One of the most important areas of research for our experts will be the need for school vouchers … Vouchers … would both improve educational performance and give the existing public school bureaucracy an incentive to make dramatic changes in their schools in order to keep parents satisfied."[27]

Therefore, the goal of the institute's support of research is not to prove whether vouchers are effective but to create arguments supporting voucher plans. Objective research is replaced by political polemics. This is most evident in the institute's efforts to effect public opinion through marketing its educational experts to the media. Using its contacts in the media, the Manhattan Institute ensures that its paid scholars will be contacted for their opinions on educational policies. This results in the frequent appearance of their experts' names in newspaper stories. The institute proudly keeps track of its media influence and lists it on its Web site under the categories of

"National Media Attention" and "Press Releases." Examples of the effec-
tiveness of these efforts can be found in daily newspapers. For instance,
when the *New York Times* reported on threatened teachers' strikes, there appeared the following comment: "'Some of the reforms that bear on teachers
are beginning to gain some traction on the ground, and teachers' organizations don't like that at all,' said Chester E. Finn Jr., an education expert at
the Manhattan Institute, a conservative research organization."[28] The
Manhattan Institute is opposed to the work of teachers' unions. When Massachusetts students protested state testing, the *New York Times* reported,
"'What we are asking for is knowledge that any student who wants a high
school diploma worth the paper it's written on should have,' said Ms.
Thernstrom, a senior fellow at the Manhattan Institute, a conservative research group. 'All other measures are subjective.'"[29] Along with George W.
Bush, the institute supports statewide testing of students. When Donald G.
and Doris Fisher, owners of The Gap clothing chain, announced that they
were providing $15 million in seed money to nationally franchise KIPP
charter schools, the *New York Times* reported, "'We've got brand-names for
everything else,' observed Chester E. Finn, an Olin Fellow at the Manhattan
Institute. 'Now we have Comer schools and Hirsch schools, and we're going
to have KIPP schools and Edison schools—You're going to be able to move
into a new city and say, "Show me the local Hirsch school." That's not a bad
idea for a modern mobile society.'"[30] The institute supports both charter
schools and privatization of public schools.

The combination of the Manhattan Institute's attempts to affect public
policy and the work of politicians is even evident in higher education. In
1998, New York City Mayor Rudy Guiliani appointed a seven-member
task force to prepare a plan for reforming the City University of New York.
Reflecting his conservative Republican views, Guiliani selected as chair of
the task force Benno Schmidt, Jr., who was head of the Edison Project—
the same private school corporation that would later select Manhattan Institute's Floyd Flake to lead its charter school division. Another member of
the task force was Heather MacDonald, a John M. Olin fellow at the
Manhattan Institute.[31]

Another method of the institute is to pay newspaper reporters to attend
so-called informational meetings. For instance, the institute, along with the
American Enterprise Institute, provided research money to Herrnstein and
Murray to write *The Bell Curve*, a book that purports to show the intellectual
inferiority of lower social classes and African Americans. After the completion of the book, the institute provided honoraria of $500—$1,500 to influential politicians and journalists to attend a seminar on Murray's research.[32]

The Manhattan Institute's association with *The Bell Curve* highlights
some of the inherent racism in conservative arguments. A group of studies used in *The Bell Curve* was supported by the Pioneer Fund, which has

been criticized for the politics of its 1937 founder, Wyckliffe Draper. Draper, a textile tycoon, was an admirer of the eugenics policies of Nazi Germany. After World War II, the Pioneer Fund provided major financial support to psychologist Arthur Jensen and physicist William Shockley, who argued that innate genetic inferiority was the cause of Black poverty and failure in school.[33]

Murray's defense for using research supported by the Pioneer Fund is stated thus: "Never mind that the relationship between the founder of the Pioneer Fund and today's Pioneer Fund is roughly analogous to that between Henry Ford and today's Ford Foundation. The charges have been made, they have wide currency, and some people will always believe that The Bell Curve rests on data concocted by neo-Nazi eugenicists."[34]

My interest is not in the statistical data used by Herrnstein and Murray to argue—I am a softheaded type who believes statistics can be manipulated to support any belief—that Whites and African Americans differ by an average of 15 IQ points. I am interested in their program recommendations, which are similar to those of other Manhattan Institute policies. For instance, Herrnstein and Murray argued that "These [differences in average IQ scores] are useful in the quest to understand why ... occupational and wage differences separate blacks and whites, or why aggressive affirmative action has produced academic apartheid in our universities."[35]

Herrnstein and Murray argued that Affirmative Action results in bringing many African American students onto college campuses who are unable to academically compete with White students. As a result, many African American students separate themselves from the rest of the student body and support Black Studies departments. This is what Herrnstein and Murray mean by "academic apartheid." Their answer to current Affirmative-Action policies is to treat people as individuals and to apply the same standards to all students. They also believe that the current form of Affirmative Action results in the dumbing down of curricula and textbooks and the spread of multiculturalism.

Herrnstein and Murray contended that the financial and social elite of society deserve their social positions because of their superior average IQs. With regard to educational policies, their concern is not with the average student, who they feel receives an adequate education commensurate with his or her IQ, but with the gifted student. In language that reflects their intellectual elitism and educational concerns, they contended:

> It needs to be said openly: The people who run the United States—create its jobs, expand its technologies, cure its sick, teach in its universities, administer its cultural and political and legal institutions—are drawn mainly from a thin layer of cognitive ability at the top .... It matters enormously not just that the people in the top few centiles of ability get to college ... or even that many of them go to elite colleges but that they are educated well.[36]

Using this reasoning, Hernstein and Murray argued for the concentration of educational programs on the needs of the gifted. Furthermore, in one of the most unusual arguments for school choice, they proposed that the federal government support school choice because parents of gifted children will be the type that will select a tougher academic program. In fact, they argued that because IQ is inherited, educational ambition is primarily "concentrated among the parents of the brightest of the brightest. Policy [referring to school choice] should make it as easy as possible for them to match up with classes that satisfy their ambitions."[37]

Although the policymakers of the Manhattan Institute are associated with these racist and elitist views, I do not want to infer that they are directly reflected in the educational policies of George W. Bush. However, the belief held by President Bush and other compassionate conservatives that the poor are poor because of their moral standards rather than economic conditions could be labeled elitist and a form of cultural imperialism. On the other hand, there is a direct connection between the educational policies of the Bush administration and the policies advocated by the Manhattan Institute.

The work of the Manhattan Institute and its effects on George W. Bush's presidency is only one example of how think tanks influence public policy. During the 1970s, compassionate conservatives' demands for school choice paralleled the extreme free-market ideas advocated by conservative think tanks. These free-market ideas included ending all government intervention in education and support of schooling and turning education over to the competition of the marketplace.

MARKETING THE EDUCATIONAL REVOLUTION: NO CHILD LEFT BEHIND

Through recruitment of scholars, distribution of educational policy statements, and access to politicians, a complex web of conservative foundations (as shown in Fig. 2.1) and think tanks were able to market the ideas that eventually found their place in the No Child Left Behind Act. Backed by this network of foundations, neoconservatives such as Chester Finn, Jr. and Diane Ravitch combined free market economics and the necessity for government standards in their public messages about education. Because they spend most of their time working for the federal government and foundations, they have achieved a presence in the popular media far beyond the capabilities of academics in universities and colleges. For instance, those familiar with "American education's newspaper of record," *Education Week,* or the op-ed pages of the *New York Times* have probably noticed educational articles frequently reporting the opinions of these two educational neoconservatives.

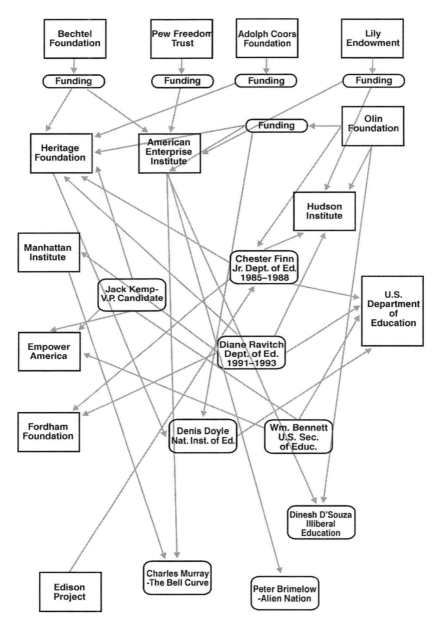

FIG. 2.1. The web of conservative think tanks in education.

Chester Finn, Jr. and Diane Ravitch founded the Educational Excellence Network in 1982 which operated out of the Hudson Institute and is now a project of the Thomas B. Fordham Foundation. The initial funding for the Educational Excellence Network came from the John M. Olin Foundation and the Andrew Mellon Foundation.[38] The Fordham Foundation was founded in 1996. In 2004, Chester Finn, Jr. was a John M. Olin Fellow at the Manhattan Institute and president of the Thomas B. Fordham Foundation. During Ronald Reagan's presidency, Finn served between 1985 and 1988 as Assistant Secretary for Research and Improvement at the U.S. Department of Education. He was also a founding partner and senior scholar with Chris Whittle's Edison Project. The Edison Project, as I discuss later, was a political force for creating charter schools and the privatization of public education.

The methods used by neoconservatives to recruit like-minded scholars are given in a 1996 letter Finn wrote to the members of the Educational Excellence Network when its work was transferred from the Hudson Institute to the Thomas B. Fordham Foundation. Finn wrote:

> Fifteen years ago this autumn, Diane Ravitch and I found ourselves on the faculties of education of two major universities: Diane at Columbia's Teachers College, I at Vanderbilt's George Peabody College. And *we found these lonely places indeed for people who believed in things like standards, content, basics, accountability and choices.*
>
> Surely, we said, *there must be at least a few other scholars and analysts who see the education world as we do and might benefit from some sort of loose-knit "network" that would foster communications, exchange information, ideas and research findings, and also offer a touch of what psychologists might term a "support group."*
>
> So Diane hosted a meeting at Teachers College and the dozen or so people who assembled there judged that this was indeed worth trying to put together. *A couple of private foundations—notably John M. Olin and Andrew Mellon—wrote modest checks to help launch our somewhat vaguely-defined venture, and off we went* [emphasis added].[39]

The home of the Educational Excellence Network, the Thomas B. Fordham Foundation, was founded in 1959, and in 1995 its board of trustees decided to focus on school issues. In 1996 Finn became the foundation's president. The foundation's offices were moved from Dayton, Ohio, to Washington, DC, and the foundation became the primary sponsor of the Educational Excellence Network. The "History" section on the Fordham Foundation's Educational Excellence Network Web site proclaims its support for the neoconservative agenda for education, "Like the EEN [Educational Excellence Network], the Foundation also welcomes the 'reinvention' of K–12 education to include such alternatives as *charter schools, contract-man-*

agement, student scholarships and other strategies for stimulating more education choices, greater competition and real consumer empowerment [emphasis added]."[40]

In 2004, the Mission statement of the Educational Excellence Network reflects the neoconservative agenda for education and the basic principles embodied in No Child Left Behind:

> The foundation's work in education seeks to advance understanding and acceptance of effective reform strategies that incorporate the following principles: the need for dramatically higher standards; an education system designed for and responsive to the needs of its users; verifiable outcomes and accountability; equality of opportunity; a solid core curriculum taught by knowledgeable, expert instructors; and educational diversity, competition, and choice.[41]

In its general mission statement, the Fordham Foundation also reflects neoconservative educational concerns in its 2004 goals:

The Foundation's Major Themes (2004):

Problems of Social Studies, History and Civics

    Curricular Content and Material

    State Standards

    Teaching controversial episodes in U.S. history

Federal Education Policy

    The No Child Left Behind Act

Charter school issues: Nationwide

    Achievement

    Financing

Charter school issues: Ohio

    Sponsorship

    Achievement

    Autonomy

Teaching and Curriculum

    Teacher Quality

    Alternative certification (teachers and principals)

    Textbooks and textbook adoption

    State math and reading standards[42]

The Educational Excellence Network flooded the market with educational policy statements and "briefings, legislation monitoring, policy analysis, and expertise to policymakers, educators, business groups, and community leaders."[43] The "Hot Topics" section of the Educational Excellence Network is dominated by the writings of Finn and Ravitch. In August 1996 two articles were offered by Finn: "Charters, Charters, and Charters" and "Making Standards Matter 1996." In June 1996 there were four articles by Finn, seven articles by Ravitch, and one by Mike Garber, and in July 1996 three articles were offered by Ravitch and one by Finn.[44]

Finn's 1996 article on charter schools provides a good example of how the media are used as part of the trickle-down theory of influencing public opinion. In early August 1996, I downloaded from the Hudson Institute's World Wide Web page Finn's article on charter schools.[45] Shortly afterward, I turned to the op-ed page of the *New York Times* and found a bold title across the top: "Beating Up on Charter Schools," by Finn, who was identified as a Fellow of the Hudson Institute and former Assistant Secretary of Education during the Reagan administration. In the article, Finn attacked the two teachers' unions—favorite targets of the right—for hindering the growth of charter schools.[46]

Finn also provides a good example of foundation-based scholars who are used by conservatives to implement their trickle-down theory of ideas. After earning his doctorate in education policy and administration at Harvard University, Finn became a professor of education at Vanderbilt University in 1981 and, while on leave from Vanderbilt, he served in a variety of government positions before becoming Assistant Secretary for Research and Improvement as well as counselor to Secretary of Education William Bennett from 1985 to 1988. After Bush replaced Reagan as president, Finn returned to Vanderbilt. In 1994, while still on leave from Vanderbilt, Finn was appointed John M. Olin Fellow at the Hudson Institute and then in 1996 became president of the Thomas Fordham Foundation.[47]

Ravitch is another foundation and government-based scholar. Ravitch served as Assistant Secretary of Education as well as counselor to the Secretary of Education from 1991 to 1993 and later became a senior research scholar at New York University and a senior Fellow at the Manhattan Institute.[48] In 1989, the Manhattan Institute established the Center for Educational Innovation for the promotion of school choice plans. The Center for Educational Innovation's World Wide Web page states that: "Our mission is to transform public education in America by shifting accountability from centralized bureaucracies to local schools and by creating systems of school choice for communities."[49]

With the support of these think tanks, Finn and Ravitch have flooded the market with neoconservative opinions about education. Besides more than 200 articles in professional and popular journals, Finn has written 10 books, including *Radical Education Reform; We Must Take Charge: Our Schools and Our Future;* and *Scholars, Dollars and Bureaucrats.* With Ravitch, Finn coauthored *What Do Our 17-Year-Olds Know?* Ravitch has also written more than 200 articles for the popular and scholarly press, and six books, including *National Standards in American Education: A Citizen's Guide 1995; The Schools We Deserve;* and *The Great School Wars: New York City, 1805–1973.*[50]

The neoconservative philosophy of Finn and Ravitch, with its combination of free market thinking and the use of government authority to impose social order, is captured in a statement by Finn in a review of a book advocating the complete separation of school and state. In reference to complete abolition of the government's role in education, Finn stated, "I don't share the author's hostility to standards, curricula and assessments set by policymakers, but I resonate with his ideas about freeing schools from state control of management and freeing families to select the education that suits them."[51]

In a similar fashion, Ravitch has argued that the academic standards of public schools declined in the 1960s and 1970s as a result of demands by civil rights groups for equality of educational opportunity and because of the capitulation of educational administrators to student rebels. Reacting to the permissiveness of the 1960s and 1970s, Ravitch believes the key to school improvement is the re-establishment of educational authority through imposition of government academic standards and achievement tests.[52]

Like William Bennett and other neoconservative critics, Finn and Ravitch argue that federal programs are controlled by a liberal elite. Despite the fact that all three of these critics held important government positions in the Office of Education, Finn and Ravitch charged that "federally funded R&D centers at elite colleges of education are a major factory for the dissemination and replenishment of the one-sided progressive philosophy."[53] Similar to other neoconservative politicians and educators, they opposed multicultural and bilingual education. They referred to the federal government's support of bilingual education as a "politicized program."[54] In contrast to their desire for immediate Americanization of immigrants, they stated, "Many bilingual educators are more interested in sustaining the ethno-linguistic, cultural, and political distinctiveness of immigrant populations than in their rapid assimilation into the mainstream."[55] This reasoning is reflected in the English Language Acquisition, Language Enhancement, and Academic Achievement Act of No Child Left Behind.

THE HERITAGE FOUNDATION
AND THE AMERICAN ENTERPRISE INSTITUTE:
MARKETING RACISM AND SCHOOL REFORM

The Heritage Foundation and the American Enterprise Institute are major disseminators of neoconservative and compassionate conservative ideas to policy makers and the public. On September 4, 2004, the Heritage Foundation, a traditional supporter of school choice, issued educational guidelines to parents that praised No Child Left Behind:

> As the summer winds down, children everywhere race to finish their summer reading assignments and parents begin their search for new notebooks, bigger backpacks, and maybe even better schools.
>
> Two years after the enactment of the No Child Left Behind Act parents have access to more information about the quality of public schools than ever before. No Child Left Behind's reporting requirements make schools more accountable to parents. Schools must issue certain specific information about achievement in reading and math, and schools that persistently fail to educate children at grade level must offer new options, such as tutoring and school choice. Armed with information and empowered by this new authority, parents are in a better position than ever before to choose where their children attend school.[56]

Eleven days after the Heritage Foundation issued its 2004 guide to parents, the American Enterprise Institute hosted a conference on No Child Left Behind where Chester Finn, Jr. and Frederick Hess, director of education policy at the American Enterprise Institute, offered their analysis of the legislation.[57] At the meeting Finn and Hess primarily complained about the legislation not completely carrying out the neoconservative education agenda and that the legislation required some internal tinkering. Finn worried that choice options supported by No Child Left Behind were lagging: "The supply of high-achieving schools, alternative options, and support programs do not keep up with the demand for choice provided by NCLB [No Child Left Behind]. More creative options need to be explored, including charter schools, home schools, cyber-schools, private schools, and inter-district transfers."[58] Hess contended that "NCLB is today too lenient about the skills and knowledge that students must acquire and too prescriptive about calendars, state improvement targets, and school sanctions. We suggest that there is a reasonable level of nationwide agreement as to what children should learn in reading and mathematics. Federal lawmakers should take advantage of that consensus."[59]

One of the organizers of the Heritage Foundation, Edwin Fuelner, referred to it as a "secondhand dealer in ideas."[60] The Heritage Foundation had its origin in a plan developed by Pat Buchanan at the request of President Nixon. Shortly after Nixon's 1972 election, Buchanan proposed the creation of an institute that would be a repository of Republican beliefs and would provide a Republican talent bank for conservative thinkers. Buchanan, along with Fuelner and Paul Weyrich, solicited $250,000 in financial support from Joseph Coors, the Colorado brewer and supporter of conservative causes. Opening its doors in 1973, the Heritage Foundation received further support from the John Olin Foundation and John Scaife, a Mellon heir and another supporter of conservative causes.[61] After the 1980 election the Heritage Foundation presented President Reagan's White House transition team with a 1,000-page volume entitled *Mandate for Change*. The volume, which summarized neoconservative thinking about a broad range of issues, including education, set the tone and direction of the Reagan administration.

Called the General Motors of conservative think tanks, the Heritage Foundation published Chester Finn, Jr. and Diane Ravitch's 1995 report on school reform in their monthly general *Policy Review*. In the same issue appeared an article by Dinesh D'Souza, who at the time was the John Olin scholar at the American Enterprise Institute.[62] D'Souza's article, "We the Slaveowners: In Jefferson's America, Were Some Men Not Created Equal?", provides an upbeat note to American slavery with the interesting conclusion that "Slavery was an institution that was terrible to endure for slaves, but it left the descendants of slaves better off in America. For this, the American Founders are owed a measure of respect and gratitude."[63]

The Heritage Foundation and the American Enterprise Institute, the two largest right-wing think tanks, provide an example of the interconnections within the neoconservative world. First, as I noted previously, both Finn and D'Souza are supported by the John M. Olin Foundation. Second, these scholars and think tanks support similar policies regarding multiculturalism and academic standards. With research and writing supported by the American Enterprise Institute and the John Olin Foundation, D'Souza's 1991 book, *Illiberal Education: The Politics of Race and Sex on Campus*, criticizes Affirmative Action and multicultural education.[64] Attacking the supposed domination of politically correct thinking on American college campuses, D'Souza argued that Affirmative Action is destructive of both minority students and the quality of education. Affirmative Action, he argued, results in colleges admitting many poorly prepared minority students. "The consequence," he claimed, is "minority students placed in 'high risk' intellectual environments where they compete against vastly better-prepared students, and where their probability of graduation is known to be low."[65] D'Souza also believes that multiculturalism and feminism are destroying liberal education by causing the replacement in college courses of significant books written by White men with inferior books written by minorities and women.

The Heritage Foundation influences politicians and the general public through the dissemination of neoconservative ideas and compassionate conservative ideas. Reflecting the compassionate conservative emphasis of the Heritage Foundation, Matthew Spalding at the 25th Annual Resource Bank Meeting of The Heritage Foundation, restated the compassionate conservative argument that religion was the basis of American society: "Republican government was possible only if the *private* virtues needed for civil society and self-government remained strong and effective. The civic responsibility and moderation of public passion also requires the moderation of private passion through the encouragement of individual morality. And the best way to encourage morality is through the flourishing of religion and the establishment of traditional moral habits."[66] He went on to state the compassionate conservative argument that the lack of government support of morality was the chief cause of American problems:

> There is a deeper problem as well. Not only does progressive liberalism deny a substantive role for morality in public life, but the extended reach of the state has forced traditional morality—the ground of the old idea of character—into a smaller and smaller private sphere. The sharp distinction between public and private, accompanied by the expansion of the governmental sphere points toward the privatization of morality. If all values are relative, and freedom now means liberation of the human will, it is hard to see any restraints on individual choice. The effect that this combination of things has had on education, religion, and the family—with the rise of illegitimacy and the breakdown of marriage—has been devastating.[67]

Praising President George W. Bush's support of faith-based organizations, Heritage Foundation's William E. Simon [Olin Foundation] Fellow in Religion and a Free Society Joseph Loconte commented on July 7, 2003, that attacks on Bush's faith-policies, "don't trump the freedom of all religious groups to live out their moral vision in a pluralistic society. Indeed, Americans of faith are likely to punish lawmakers who attack their religious institutions. That fact alone might, in the end, inspire a little more charity toward the nation's Good Samaritans."[68]

In contrast to the dissemination role of the Heritage Foundation, the American Enterprise Institute focuses on supporting neoconservative scholarship. Originally organized in 1943 to educate the public about business, the American Enterprise Institute dramatically changed in the 1960s under the leadership of William J. Baroody, who applied the concepts of Austrian economics to the world of ideas. Baroody believed there existed a liberal monopoly of ideas. Baroody argued that "a free society can tolerate some degree of concentration in the manufacture of widgets. But the day it approaches a monopoly in idea formation, that is its death knell."[69]

Baroody proposed creating a free market of ideas by breaking the liberal monopoly through the establishment of conservative think tanks. Once competition was created, he believed, the invisible hand of the marketplace would determine the value of particular ideas. During the early 1970s, Melvin Laird, Secretary of Defense in the Nixon administration, kicked off a $25 million fund raising campaign for the American Enterprise Institute in a Pentagon dining room. By the 1980s, the institute had a staff of 150 and an annual budget of more than $10 million.

In the 1990s, evidence of the American Enterprise Institute's success at introducing conservative thinking into the marketplace of ideas is illustrated in Peter Brimelow's afterword to his anti-immigration book *Alien Nation*. Brimelow, writer for the conservative *Forbes* magazine, recalled in his afterword to the paperback edition of his book an incident at an American Enterprise Institute ceremony in which Judge Robert Bork commented, "We at [the American Enterprise Institute] are grateful to you for drawing fire away from Charles Murray."[70] (The other author of *The Bell Curve*, Richard Herrnstein, died shortly after completion of the manuscript.) Brimelow commented about Bork's remarks, "Later … I got a call from Murray himself, Bork's colleague at [the American Enterprise Institute] … curious to see how I was holding up [from the stormy reaction to the publication of *Alien Nation*]."[71] Also, reflecting the web of conservative connections, Brimelow acknowledged intellectual and financial support from the Cato Institute and William F. Buckley of the conservative *National Review*, where Brimelow had originally published his immigration argument in a 1992 cover story.[72]

Brimelow's book supports right-wing and racist ideas regarding immigration. In *Alien Nation* Brimelow expressed concern about the decreasing percentage of Whites in the U.S. population. Arguing that U.S. citizens have a legitimate interest in the racial composition of their population, Brimelow commented, "The American nation of 1965, nearly 90 percent white, were explicitly promised that the new immigration policy would not shift the country's racial balance. But it did … [and] it seems to me that they have a right to insist that it be shifted back."[73] The result of shifting racial patterns, Brimelow claims, is a destruction of national unity and cultural homogeneity. To solve this problem, he proposed closing the gates to immigrants for several years and, when they are reopened, using racial balance and labor market needs as criteria for selecting new immigrants.

Brimelow argues that the shift in racial and cultural composition of the population resulted in strong support for Affirmative Action, bilingual education, and multicultural education. These policies, he feels, put Whites at an unfair disadvantage in the labor market and are causing a disintegration of traditional U.S. culture. Like other scholars of the right, Brimelow wants multiculturalism replaced with Americanization programs based on traditional American values and the implementation of an English-only national language policy. In Brimelow's words, "All diversion of public funds to promote 'diversity,' 'multiculturalism' and foreign-language retention must be struck down as subversive."[74]

NEOCONSERVATIVES, BUSINESS, AND EDUCATIONAL STANDARDS

No Child Left Behind's mandate for states to create educational standards can be traced back to the 1983 report *A Nation at Risk*. After founding the Education Excellence Network in 1981, Finn and Ravitch recalled that their efforts received little public attention until the appearance of *A Nation at Risk*. "To put it mildly," they remembered, "this bombshell [*A Nation at Risk*] awakened parents, educators, governors, legislators, and the press .... Its warning of 'a rising tide of mediocrity' helped launch what came to be called the excellence movement, which included a mass of other commissions, studies, and reports."[75]

Issued by the Reagan administration, *A Nation at Risk* contains the unproven and often-repeated claim that the poor quality of schools was responsible for the difficulties U.S. corporations were experiencing competing in international markets. The report opened with alarming language: "Our nation is at risk. Our once unchallenged preeminence in commerce, industry, science and technological innovation is being overtaken by competitors throughout the world." Dramatically claiming that the poor quality of U.S. schools threatened the future of the nation, the report stated: "If an unfriendly foreign power had attempted to impose on America the mediocre educational performance that exists today, we might well have viewed it as an act of war."[76]

The traditional Republican approach to educational policies is to link economic performance with the quality of public schools. In this tradition, the primary role of the schools is to educate workers—called human capital—who will improve economic efficiency and technological development. During the 1950s, the National Manpower Council played a major role in defining the human capital policies of the Republican party. Founded in 1951 in response to the labor needs of the Cold War, the National Manpower Council, reflecting the technological needs of the Cold War, recommended in its first report in 1951 that Selective Service deferments should be used "to insure a continuous supply of college-trained people whose general education and specialized knowledge are essential to the nation's civilian and military strength."[77] In 1953, the council issued "A Policy for Scientific and Professional Manpower," warning that the Soviet Union's totalitarian methods were forcing large numbers of students to study science and engineering, which would make the Soviet Union superior in technology and military weaponry. The problem facing the United States was persuading more talented youth to enter technological fields.[78]

The Soviet launching of Sputnik in 1957 seemed to confirm the warnings of the National Manpower Council. Within a month of the Sputnik launch, President Eisenhower called on the U.S. school system to educate more scientists and engineers to match the large numbers being graduated by the Soviet educational system. "My scientific advisers," Eisenhower declared, "place [the shortage of scientists and engineers] above all other immediate tasks of producing missiles, of developing new techniques in the armed services."[79] Convinced that the education of more scientists and engineers was the key to winning the Cold War, Eisenhower proposed the National Defense Education Act, which was passed by Congress in 1958. It is ironic that when one considers later Republican objections to federal involvement in education, the National Defense Education Act—with its scholarships, student loans, support for the development of new math and science curricula for public schools, and aid for recruiting more teachers—actually was one of the first major involvements in modern times of the federal government in public education. Republican concerns with human capital development continued into the 1970s, when President Richard Nixon supported federal grants for career education programs. Nixon hoped that career education would create a closer alignment of the public school curriculum with the needs of the labor market. Within this framework, public schools would convince students to think about education in relation to a future job; to focus their learning on the skills required for that job; and then, after graduation, to move smoothly into the labor market.[80]

Therefore, *A Nation at Risk* was not a sharp break from previous Republican considerations of schooling as an important part of economic planning. The emphasis on school improvement as a means of strengthening the position of U.S. corporations in world markets continued in later reports. *A Nation Prepared: Teachers for the 21st Century* (1986), issued by the Carnegie Forum on Education and the Economy, blamed economic conditions on the low quality of American teachers who were preparing workers for the new global economy. *A Nation Prepared* proposed a redirection for American schools from preparation for mass-production industries to preparation for knowledge-based industries.[81]

The report urged schools to replace the repetitive learning methods needed for mass production with learning methods that develop higher order thinking. According to the report, these older instructional methods could be packaged easily in textbooks that provided instructional guides for teachers. In the new world economy, the report claimed, the development of higher order thinking requires workers who are prepared for nonroutine and unexpected tasks. For the writers of *A Nation Prepared*, meeting the needs of the world economy required the abandonment of traditional methods of instruction, school organization, and teacher training. Although *A Nation Prepared* anticipated later demands by neoconservatives and New Democrats to create "break the mold" schools, *Action for Excellence* (1983) drew governors and corporate leaders into the snowballing school reform movement. *Action for Excellence* was issued by the Education Commission of the States' Task Force on Education for Economic Growth, which was composed of representatives of major corporations and governors. Its funding came from some of the largest corporations, including IBM and Xerox, whose chief executives—Louis V. Gerstner, Jr., and David Kearns— later worked with neoconservatives on school reform. The involvement of governors demonstrated the political grip of school reform. By 1989, neoconservative Gov. Lamar Alexander and New Democrat Gov. Bill Clinton were working for school reform.

Involvement of business in public school reform highlights a major difference between adherents of Austrian economics and neoconservatives. To advocates of free markets there are major dangers in corporations using government to protect their place in the market. Austrian economists worry as much about business control of government, as they do about bureaucratic control of the marketplace. In contrast, neoconservatives accept business involvement in government along with the government's role in exercising moral and social authority. The increasing role of business is indicated by a statement in *Action for Excellence*: "If the business community gets more involved in both the design and delivery of education, we are going to become more competitive as an economy."[82]

In 1994, Gerstner, CEO and chairman of IBM, explained that he "wanted to go beyond traditional business partnerships that enhance schools by providing equipment, mentors, or increased opportunities .... While these generous efforts may brighten the picture for a few children, they do not change 'the system.'"[83] Claiming that his interest in educational reform was "fueled by intense anger, and frustration," Gerstner emphatically asserted that "You know that most young applicants are not qualified to do today's more intellectually demanding jobs, let alone tomorrow's."[84]

Neoconservatives are not alone in supporting business involvement in public schools. In 1996, President Bill Clinton welcomed 49 corporate chiefs and 40 governors to a national education summit held at IBM's conference center at Palisades, New York. Cohosting the event were Gerstner and Republican Gov. Tommy Thompson. Both neoconservatives and New Democrats welcomed the summit meeting's emphasis on creating national and state academic standards.[85]

Two basic themes emerged from the interplay among neoconservatives, business people, and New Democrats. One was that low academic standards were resulting in poorly prepared students and inadequately trained teachers. The correction of these problems, it was argued, could be achieved through increased academic requirements for students and for the certification of teachers. In addition, student achievement could be improved by requiring statewide or national achievement tests for promotion between grades and graduation. The same concept was applied to teachers. The result was that the late 1980s and early 1990s became a heyday for the creation of statewide student and teacher tests. The proposals contained in *A Nation Prepared* eventually resulted in the creation of the National Board for Professional Teaching Standards, which developed a national teacher's examination and began awarding national teacher certification in 1993.[86]

The second theme was that public schools needed to be redesigned to meet the needs of the "Information Age." Advocates of school choice could now claim that competition would produce new types of schools. In addition, the concern with redesigning schools provided a rationale for charter and for-profit schools.

Neoconservative assumptions about the failure of public schools are being challenged. Michael Lind calls the charge that public schools are academic failures one of the "three conservative hoaxes" of modern times. Lind wrote, "Thanks to a decade and a half of well-coordinated conservative propaganda, many Americans have been persuaded that America's public schools are miserable failures and that American students are among the worst in the industrialized world. Those who believe these assertions, it turns out, have been misled."[87] In *The Manufactured Crisis: Myths, Fraud, and the Attack on America's Public Schools*, David Berliner and Bruce Biddle argue that the conservative hoax began in the 1980s, when the Reagan administration issued the report *A Nation at Risk*, which claimed the American economy was failing because of its public schools. Countering *A Nation at Risk*, Berliner and Biddle provided statistics showing that U.S. students taking courses similar to those of students in other countries, such as Japan and Germany, do as well or, in some cases, better, and that it is the comprehensiveness of the student body in U.S. public schools that tends to lower overall scores. Berliner and Biddle argued that not until the appearance of *A Nation at Risk* did neoconservatives such as Bennett, Finn, and Lynne Cheney launch their attacks on public schools.[88]

GOALS 2000: ON THE ROAD TO NO CHILD LEFT BEHIND

George W. Bush's father, President George Bush, favored strong federal involvement in education. In this respect, George W. is carrying on his father's tradition, with the major difference being George W.'s closer affiliation with religiously-oriented compassionate conservatives. His father's commitment to federal involvement in education is exemplified by

Goals 2000, which also highlights the crisscrossing lines between the educational policies of neoconservatives and Bill Clinton and John Kerry's New Democrats. President George Bush officially inaugurated Goals 2000 at the President's Education Summit With Governors at the University of Virginia on September 27, 1989. The governors were formally represented by the National Governors' Association, which was chaired by Republican Governor, and later Secretary of Education, Lamar Alexander. The vice chairman was Gov. Clinton.

Emphasizing the themes of human capital, academic standards, and reinvention of schools, the joint statement issued in 1989 by the President and the National Governors' Association reiterated what was becoming an unquestioned assumption: "As a nation we must have an educated work force, second to none, in order to succeed in an increasingly competitive world economy."[89] Linking human capital to national academic standards, the joint statement declared: "We believe that the time has come, for the first time in U.S. history, to establish clear national performance goals, goals that will make us internationally competitive."[90]

A revolution, according to this Bush administration, would take place with the implementation of Goals 2000, which were laced with references to "productive employment," "first in the world in science and mathematics," and "global economy"; the goals and the strategy for the implementation of Goals 2000 promised a new day for American schools. To help implement Goals 2000, President Bush appointed Lamar Alexander as Secretary of Education in 1991 and the ever-present Ravitch as Assistant Secretary of Education in charge of the Office of Educational Research and Improvement. Alexander had built his political career in Tennessee with the promise that educational reform would improve the state's economy. In 1996, Alexander would be a candidate for the Republican Presidential nomination. With claims that education was the key to the economic success of the United States, President Bush, with the aid of Lamar Alexander and Diane Ravitch, released on April 18, 1991, a plan for implementing Goals 2000: *America 2000: An Education Strategy*. Without any proof that the school quality was the cause of U.S. problems in international trade or that school reform would improve the economy, Bush, using the language of human capital, stated, "Down through history, we've defined resources as soil and stone, land and the riches buried beneath. No more. Our greatest national resource lies within ourselves ... the capacity of the human mind .... If we want to keep America competitive in the coming century, ... we must accept responsibility for educating everyone among us."[91]

Speaking to the concerns of corporate leaders who did not want school reform to cost a bundle, and to neoconservatives who believed the public school monopoly and bureaucracy were the problem, and not money, Bush claimed that a 33% increase in educational spending since 1981 had not resulted in a 33% improvement in schools' performance. "Dollar bills don't educate students," Bush asserted. "To those who want to see real improvement in American education, I say: There will be no renaissance without revolution."[92]

The heart of the implementation strategy was an "Accountability Package," which would eventually, in an altered form, appear as part of No Child Left Behind. The first part of the accountability package, and dear to the hearts of neoconservatives, was the creation of world-class standards by a national education goals panel that would "incorporate both knowledge and skills, to ensure that, when they leave school, young Americans are prepared for further study and the work force."[93] The second step was writing American achievement tests based on the world-class standards created by the national education goals panel. These voluntary tests were "to foster good teaching and learning as well as to monitor student progress."[94] Disappointing both compassionate conservatives and neoconservatives, Bush proposed that school choice be limited to public schools.

The major components of George Bush's educational strategies were national academic standards, national achievement tests, and corporate involvement in American schools. All of these proposals were made in the context of improving the competitive edge of American corporations in international markets. As David Hornbeck, former Maryland state superintendent, commented at the time, "For the first time in American history, what is good for kids and what is good for business coincides almost on a one-for-one basis."[95]

STANDARDS AND TESTS: THE POLITICS OF CULTURE

It is surprising that no one seemed to give much thought to the ideological problems of creating standards and tests. Even in mathematics, a field often thought of as politically neutral, there exist major differences over what should be taught and how it should be taught. When the "New Math," as it was called in the early 1960s, was introduced, its emphasis on teaching arithmetic to elementary school children using set and number theories encountered a storm of protest from conservative parents who wanted arithmetic instruction to use traditional methods, such as memorization of the multiplication table.[96]

In the development of national standards and tests in the 1990s, history has proved to be the most politically contentious subject. No Child Left behind specifically addresses this issue by providing grants for the teaching of Traditional American History (Item 2 of the legislative summary given in chapter 1). Traditional American history refers to the content of history prior to emphasis on social and cultural history that occurred in the 1960s. Specifically, No Child Left Behind states that grants are to be given

(1) to carry out activities to promote the teaching of traditional American history in elementary schools and secondary schools as a separate academic subject (*not as a component of social studies*); and

(2) for the development, implementation, and strengthening of programs to teach traditional American history as a separate academic subject (*not as a component of social studies*) within elementary school and secondary school curricula.[97]

Because history is shaped by and contains political values, the debate over history standards reflects broad divisions in political ideas. In 1986, foreshadowing the national standards debate over history, California Superintendent of Public Instruction Bill Honig appointed Ravitch, who at the time was an adjunct professor at Teachers College of Columbia University, and Charlotte Crabtree, a professor of education at the University of California, Los Angeles, to a panel to rewrite the state social studies curriculum. In 1987, California officials approved a framework for the teaching of history that was primarily written by Ravitch and Crabtree.[98]

The controversy over the California framework centered on its portrayal of the United States as a land of immigrants sharing a common set of values. The debate occurred in New York, with Arthur Schlesinger, Jr. and Ravitch playing major roles.[99] The dispute highlights significant differences regarding the teaching and interpretation of U.S. history. For neoconservatives, the major purpose of teaching history is to create national unity by teaching a common set of political and social values. These common values, according to the neoconservative approach, should be based on the beliefs underlying American institutions. In Schlesinger's words, "For better or worse, the White Anglo-Saxon Protestant tradition was for two centuries—and in crucial respects still is—the dominant influence on American culture and society .... The language of the new nation, its laws, its institutions, its political ideas, its literature, its customs, its precepts, its prayers, primarily derived from Britain."[100] Using similar words, Honig stated that "This country has been able to celebrate pluralism but keep some sense of the collective that holds us together .... Democracy has certain core ideas—freedom of speech, law, procedural rights, the way we deal with each other."[101]

From a conservative perspective, teaching core values would reduce racial and ethnic strife in U.S. society and ensure the perpetuation of traditional American values. Within this framework the content of U.S. history should emphasize the common struggles and benefits received from U.S. institutions by the diverse cultural groups composing its population. The study of differing cultures in the United States, such as Native American and African, should emphasize tolerance and unity under common institutions. Similar to Dinesh D'Souza's interpretation, slavery is presented as a negative institution that developed in an otherwise positive society which, in the end, provided a better life for the descendants of enslaved Africans.

The major objections to the neoconservative interpretation of U.S. history come from individuals who practice the politics of cultural identity. One objection to the California framework came from Nathan Huggins, a Harvard professor of African American studies and history. Huggins warned, "A stress on 'common culture' turns history into a tool of national unity, mandated principally by those anxious about national order and coherence."[102] There was outrage among some African Americans, Mexican Americans, and Native Americans at the concept of the United States being a land of immigrants. All three groups could claim to be unwilling members of U.S. society who had been forced into participation by slavery and conquest. From this perspective, the history of the United States is marked by White violence against Africans, Mexicans, Asians, and Native Americans. This racial violence brings into question the worth of White Anglo-Saxon values undergirding American institutions. Stanford University professor of African and Afro-American studies Sylvia Wynter argued that the California history framework "does not move outside the conceptual field of our present essentially Euro-American cultural model." The framework, she argued, did not provide a means for understanding the plight of minority groups in the United States. Wynter asked:

> How did the dispossession of the indigenous peoples, their subordination, and the mass enslavement of the people of Black African descent come to seem "just and virtuous" actions to those who affected them? How does the continuance of this initial dispossession, in the jobless, alcohol-ridden reservations, the jobless drug and crime ridden inner cities ... still come to seem to all of us, as just, or at the very least, to be in the nature of things?[103]

Joyce King, then a professor of education at Santa Clara University and one of the leading critics of the California framework, was particularly disturbed by the "we are all immigrants" interpretation of U.S. history. King called this approach a "dysconscious racism ... an impaired consciousness or a distorted way of thinking about race ... [that] tacitly accepts dominant White norms and privileges."[104] The California framework, she argued, presents a triumphant chronological history, which recognizes the unfortunate conquest of Indians and enslavement of Africans, progressing to an inevitable point when all groups are able to acquire the supposed "superior" values of White Anglo-Saxon society. In this context, national unity requires that all cultural groups recognize the advantages of White Anglo-Saxon traditions.

The California controversy foreshadowed later discussions about the politics of knowledge. After Ravitch's appointment in 1991 as Assistant Secretary of Education in charge of the Office of Educational Research and Improvement, Charlotte Crabtree's National Center for History in Schools received a joint award of $1.6 million from Ravitch's office and the National Endowment of the Humanities to develop national history standards. At the time, the National Endowment for the Humanities was headed by Lynne Cheney (her husband was famed neoconservative and later Vice President Dick Cheney), who shared a common philosophy about the humanities with her predecessor, William Bennett.

To the horror of Ravitch and Cheney, the first set of national standards in history contained teaching examples that, in Cheney's words, "make it sound as if everything in America is wrong and grim." Cheney complained that the teaching examples contained 17 references to the Ku Klux Klan and 19 references to McCarthyism, whereas there was no mention of Paul Revere, Thomas Edison, and other "politically incorrect White males."[105] The teaching examples were done outside the neoconservative political fold by Carol Gluck, a professor of history at Columbia University. Using what she called a democratic process, Gluck spent 2 years meeting with more than 6,000 parents, teachers, businesspeople, and school administrators.[106] Outraged, Cheney founded a Washington-based Committee to Review National Standards to apply political pressure for a revision of the history standards.

In 1995, the National Center for History in the Schools announced that it was revising the history standards and teaching examples. Claiming a victory, Ravitch said she hoped that "we can declare this particular battlefront in the culture wars to be ended."[107] In reporting Ravitch's statement, Karen Diegmueller explained that Ravitch was "a panelist who not only had criticized the documents but had commissioned their creation when she served as an assistant secretary in the U.S. Department of Education."[108] Diegmueller reported that the criticisms of the history standards were primarily from neoconservatives who contended, in Diegmueller's words, that "the standards undercut the great figures that traditionally have dominated the landscape of history and portray the United States and the West as oppressive regimes that have victimized women, minorities, and third-world countries."[109] What the critics wanted, Diegmueller wrote, was a history that emphasized U.S. accomplishments and provided students with uplifting ideals. With a cynical tone, Diegmueller opened a later *Education Week* article with these words: "Timbuktu has disappeared. Pearl Harbor has ascended. George Washington is in; Eleanor Roosevelt is out. And names and places like Joseph McCarthy and Seneca Falls, NY, whose prominence irked critics ... have been allotted one mention apiece."[110] She also reported an attempt to give a more upbeat tone to the introductions to the 10 eras of U.S. history delimited by the standards.

In 2004, the Thomas B. Fordham Institute published Diane Ravitch's *A Consumer's Guide to High School History Textbooks*.[111] This book contains a review by a group of scholars of 13 American and World History textbooks written for senior high schools. Among a variety of things, the scholars were asked to examine whether or not the textbooks were biased. None of the reviews found a *conservative* bias to the books. However, some books were charged with being "left-liberal" and "leftist." For instance, Morton Keller, Spector Professor of History Emeritus at Brandeis University, asserts that Gary B. Nash's *American Odyssey: The United States in the Twentieth Century* is "the most biased and partisan of the texts reviewed here: unabashed in its politically (if not historically) correct definition of diversity, and in its adherence to a left-liberal view of modern America."[112] Another reviewer, Edward J. Renehan, Jr., author of *The Kennedys at War* charges that there is "a leftist political bias" to Gerald A. Danzer, J. Jorge Klor de Alva, Larry S. Krieger, Louise E. Wilson, and Nancy Woloch's *The Americans*. Renehan states, "The book's section on HUAC [House Un-American Activities Committee], Senator Joseph McCarthy, etc. could easily have been written by Paul Robeson [noted Communist of the period]."[113] Ravitch reports that Jeffrey Mirel, Associate Dean for Academic Affairs at the University of Michigan, found the *American Odyssey* to have

> a "deeply pessimistic" view, in which the nation's failures consistently outweigh its commitment to its ideals. Mirel faults Nash for never making his interpretation explicit; the book "proceeds as if it is giving a fair and balanced picture of American history, but its tendency to accentuate the nation's flaws belies that impression." Mirel criticizes Nash's text for its extensive attention to McCarthyism and its relative neglect of the nature of the Soviet regime, which was an important contextual element in this era. Without this context, the controversies over spies and treason are incomprehensible. Nash even chides President Truman for painting "too harsh a picture" of life under Communist rule. Mirel concludes that "it is difficult to judge a book as even-handed and fair that devotes so much time to violations of people's civil liberties [in the U.S.] ... but does not even mention the millions of deaths under Soviet Communism."[114]

The culture wars surrounding the history standards mirrored broad differences in political values between neoconservatives and the left. What is important to note is that these differences went beyond the usual concept of politics to include issues of knowledge. The politics of knowledge involve questions such as: Who should determine the political values taught to students? What political values should be taught to students? What is the relation between the political beliefs of politicians and the political ideas presented to students? The neoconservative criticism of the history standards underscores the general attempt by right-wing think tanks to influence the minds of citizens.

FOR-PROFIT AND CHARTER SCHOOLS

No Child Left Behind supports for-profit education companies and public charter schools. In many ways, the legislation is a major step in the privat-

ization of the public school system. Scattered throughout No Child Left Behind are provisions to support for-profit companies. For instance, the
legislation states that assistance to schools requiring improvement because
of low test scores can be provided by a "for-profit agency."[115] Under the
Reading First section, reading and literacy partnerships can be established
between school districts and for-profit companies.[116] Also, state and local
school districts are provided funds to contract with for-profit companies to
provide advance placement courses and services; to reform teacher and
principal certification; to recruit "highly qualified teachers, including specialists in core academic subjects, principals, and pupil services personnel";
to improve science and mathematics curriculum and instruction; "to develop State and local teacher corps or other programs to establish, expand,
and enhance teacher recruitment and retention efforts"; to integrate
"proven teaching practices into instruction"; for professional development
programs; to provide services to teachers of limited English proficient students and for developing and implementing programs for limited English
proficient students; to create and expand community technology centers;
to accredit basic education of Indian children in Bureau of Indian Affairs
Schools; and to train prospective teachers in advanced technology.[117]

Also, charter schools receive direct support from No Child Left Behind.
As part of a public school system, public charter schools can be managed by
a private company which charges a fee to the local school district. In this sit-
uation, the public charter school is non-profit, but the company, such as the
Edison Schools (originally called the Edison Project), operating a public
charter school earns a profit through the fees it charges the school district.
No Child Left Behind provides the following definition of charter schools:

> (1) CHARTER SCHOOL.—The term "charter school" means a public school
> that—
>
> (A) in accordance with a specific State statute authorizing the granting of
> charters to schools, is exempt from significant State or local rules that in-
> hibit the flexible operation and management of public schools, but not
> from any rules relating to the other requirements of this paragraph;
>
> (B) is created by a developer as a public school, or is adapted by a developer
> from an existing public school, and is operated under public supervision
> and direction;[118]

In addition, the legislation includes in its definition that public charter schools must comply with state and federal regulations regarding discrimination.

There are a number of parts of No Child Left Behind that support the
idea of charter schools. For instance, students in schools identified as needing improvement based on test scores can choose a public charter school.[119]

Students in schools that fail to improve after being identified as needing improvement can transfer to a charter school.[120] Charter schools can be funded as part of a dropout prevention program.[121] Financial support is provided for charter schools in the legislation's Title V–Promoting Informed Parental Choice and Innovative Programs, Part B–Public Charter Schools, which states:

> It is the purpose of this subpart to increase national understanding of the charter schools model by—
>
> (1) providing financial assistance for the planning, program design, and initial implementation of charter schools;
>
> (2) evaluating the effects of such schools, including the effects on students, student academic achievement, staff, and parents;
>
> (3) expanding the number of high-quality charter schools available to students across the Nation; and
>
> (4) encouraging the States to provide support to charter schools for facilities financing in an amount more nearly commensurate to the amount the States have typically provided for traditional public schools.[122]

In part, the charter and for-profit school movement originated in efforts by neoconservatives to create competition. Ideally, from the perspective of many neoconservatives, the educational marketplace would involve competition between for-profit schools. The assumption is that the profit motive will drive institutions to create the best educational product that will appeal to parents. Educational entrepreneur Chris Whittle came up with the idea of franchising for-profit schools. Whittle was counting on a government voucher system that would allow parents to choose between private and public schools. Whittle wanted to capture some of this voucher money by designing a conservative and technologically advanced school that could be franchised across the country.

Politically Whittle is a neoconservative. He made his position in the culture wars evident when he convinced the Federal Express Corporation to help fund the publication of Schlesinger's attack on multicultural education, *The Disuniting of America*.[123] Schlesinger's book carries the imprint of Whittle Direct Books and has full-page ads for Federal Express scattered through the text. Reminiscent of William Simon, Whittle tried to ensure that Schlesinger's educational ideas received a wide audience by sending free copies to business leaders around the country.

Whittle's political views are exemplified by his selection of the conservative president of Yale University, Benno Schmidt, to head his for-profit school enterprise. Whittle made the decision to hire Schmidt over food and drinks at a party in the ultraexclusive Hamptons on Long Island. Offered an annual salary of about $1 million, Schmidt left Yale in 1992 to head what was called the Edison Project. As one of the consultants on the project, Whittle hired Chester Finn, Jr.[124]

Part of Whittle's plans went awry when the 1992 election of President Clinton seemed to doom any chance of government-financed public–private school vouchers. In addition, Whittle faced money problems that eventually led to his withdrawal from the project. At this point, the Edison Project moved from Whittle's home base in Knoxville, Tennessee, to its present location in New York City.[125]

Without public–private school vouchers, the only hope for the Edison Project was to franchise private schools that were dependent on tuition income or to seek some other form of public support. The opportunity for public support came, according to *New York* magazine reporter James Traub, when "governors William Weld of Massachusetts and Buddy Roemer of Colorado contacted Schmidt in the fall of 1992 that they would like to find a way to bring Edison into the public schools in their states. Both states went on to pass 'charter school' laws that permit states and school systems to award contracts to … private contractors."[126] With charter schools, the operation of for-profit schools is a possibility.

For many neoconservatives, charter schools are a method for getting around the power of the educational bureaucracy. At the Hudson Institute, Chester Finn, Jr., with support from the Pew Charitable Trusts, conducted a major national study of charter schools. In an initial report in 1996, Finn, along with his colleagues Bruno Manno and Louann Bierlein, praised charter schools because "they serve the public in a different way, more like the voluntary institutions of 'civil society' than the compulsory/monopolistic organs of government."[127]

The continued support of competition and charter schools appears in the 2004 Republican Platform which states, "President Bush, Republican governors, and members of Congress have worked to expand parental choice and *encourage competition* by providing parents with information on their child's school, *increasing the number of charter schools*, and expanding education savings accounts for use from kindergarten through college [emphasis added]."[128]

Edison schools are an example of a leading for-profit education company. In 2004, the company claimed, "Edison Charter Schools is the nation's largest and most successful network of independent public charter schools in terms of student achievement gains. Edison Charter Schools serves approximately 25,000 students and 29 non-profit charter school boards in 14 states and D.C."[129] Also, Edison Schools has expanded its operation into Great Britain. Its company profile states:

> In 2004-2005, Edison Schools will serve more than 250,000 students in 20 states, the District of Columbia, and the United Kingdom. Approximately 71,000 students will attend 157 district partnership and charter schools managed by Edison; approximately 67,500 students will participate in Edison's

Newton Learning after-school and summer school programs and approximately 42,000 students will attend Newton Learning SES programs; approximately 75,000 students will benefit from achievement management solutions provided by Edison's Tungsten Learning; and 15,000 students will be served by Edison Schools UK programs.[130]

CONCLUSION

In summary, No Child Left Behind embodies the ideologies of compassionate conservatives and neoconservatives. Conservative think tanks marketed their ideas about school choice by financing conservative-oriented research and by using public relations methods to influence media, politicians, and the general public. However, the work of neoconservative think tanks also highlights an important difference between neoconservatives and compassionate conservatives. Compassionate conservatives are hesitant about the government imposing national academic standards and testing. They want to rely on the authority of God. School choice would provide compassionate conservatives with this opportunity. In contrast, neoconservatives, such as Doyle, Finn, and Ravitch, believe that school choice will create more efficient ways of implementing government-established national academic goals and standards.

It is important to emphasize that a conscious effort is being made to disseminate ideas and influence public opinion by conservative think tanks, such as the Manhattan Institute, the Heritage Foundation, the Thomas B. Fordham Foundation and the American Enterprise Institute. Their influence is the result of calculated planning by conservative intellectuals and businesspeople. In 1986, at a celebration of the accomplishments of the Heritage Foundation, President Reagan recognized the importance of conservative attempts to influence public opinion. After paying homage to Austrian economists Friedrich Hayek and Ludwig von Mises, Reagan recalled the argument made by Richard Weaver in the 1948 book *Ideas Have Consequences*. Reagan told those celebrating of the work of the Heritage Foundation: "It goes back to what Richard Weaver had said and what Heritage is all about. Ideas do have consequences, rhetoric is policy, and words are action."[131]

Chapter 3

New Democrats
and No Child Left Behind

"So my first message is let's fix public education," Pennsylvania's Democratic Governor Edward Rendell told the panel on Creating Higher-Skill, Higher-Wage Jobs at the 2004 Democratic National Convention, "and the only way we do that is to get a president who believes in public education and John Kerry does." Governor Rendell went on to remind the panel that No Child Left Behind was a bipartisan effort, "You know, when Teddy Kennedy [Democratic Senator Edward Kennedy of Massachusetts] stood with George Bush and announced No Child Left Behind, I supported it because I believe our kids do need to be tested once a year, but only if after we test them we have the dollars to remediate."[1]

Democratic support of No Child Left Behind is based on the belief—and as yet unproven—that educational standards, testing, and charter school provisions would help American workers and the American economy compete in the global marketplace. However, there are sharp differences between neoconservatives and those calling themselves "New Democrats" over the role of privatization in government reform. The New Democratic movement, as I will explain in the next section of this chapter, originated in the 1990s from the work of the Democratic Leadership Council. While neoconservatives support privatization of government services, including a reliance on for-profit private companies to provide public school services, New Democrats want to make government services more responsive to citizen desires through, for instance, parental choice of public schools and public charter schools. New Democrats do not publicly support those provisions in No Child Left Behind that are dear to the hearts of religiously oriented Republicans, such as school prayer, Boy Scouts, and teaching traditional American history. In fact, they are often critical of the blend of religious beliefs and educational policies that characterize some Republicans. Speaking on the same panel as Governor Rendell, Professor Rosabeth Moss Kanter of the Harvard Business School referred to "Senator Kerry, hopefully President Kerry" before calling for a national science and math education policy and expressing her worry that, "high school biology is being held captive to politics right now because of debates about things like the teaching of creationism. Can you imagine our scientists competing in the world if they're taught not science, but local politics driven by the politics of religions?"[2]

During the 2004 presidential campaign, Democrats criticized the lack of funding of No Child Left Behind and not the details of the legislation. For instance, the 2004 Democratic National Platform states, "When President Bush signed the No Child Left Behind Act, he said the right things—asking more from our schools and pledging to give them the resources to get the job done. And then he promptly broke his word, providing schools $27 billion less than he had promised, literally leaving millions of children behind."[3]

Blueprint Magazine, a publication of the Democratic Leadership Council, compared the 2004 presidential candidates on educational issues. Again, there is no criticism of No Child Left Behind, but there is criticism of President Bush's handling of the legislation:

> George Bush has set back the cause of education reform with bureaucratic bungling of the No Child Left behind Act. He has no plan to help every child succeed, or make sure every teacher is qualified. The Kerry and Edwards education plan will finish the job of education reform by paying teachers better and demanding more in return; providing more after-school programs; breaking up big troubled high schools, and helping million more students graduate high school.[4]

THE NEW DEMOCRATS

Democratic support of the accountability, standards, and charter school provisions of No Child Left originated in the work of former President Bill Clinton and the Democratic Leadership Council which Clinton chaired from 1991 to 1992. Formed in 1985 as an unofficial party organization, the council developed plans to move the Democratic party to the center of the political spectrum and coined the term "New Democrats." The Council formed a think tank, the Progressive Policy Institute, to support scholars formulating the new centrist political position. Both groups continue to be important in formulating Democratic Party policies.

The Democratic Leadership Council offers the following description of its centrist activities:

> The Democratic Leadership Council [DLC] is an idea center, catalyst, and national voice for a reform movement that is reshaping American politics by

moving it beyond the old left-right debate. Under the leadership of founder and CEO Al From, the DLC seeks to define and galvanize popular support for a new public philosophy built on *progressive ideals, mainstream values, and innovative, non-bureaucratic, market-based solutions*. At its heart are three principles: promoting opportunity for all; demanding responsibility from everyone; and fostering a new sense of community [my emphasis].[5]

As indicated in the above, the New Democrats are in agreement with neoconservatives regarding "non bureaucratic" and "market-based solutions."

The think tank of the New Democrats, the Progressive Policy Institute (PPI) is described in the same anti-bureaucratic language. The Institute distinguishes itself from neoconservative efforts to "dismantle government." It claims to be offering a "third way" in American politics.

Defining the Third Way

PPI's mission arises from the belief that America is ill-served by an obsolete left-right debate that is out of step with the powerful forces re-shaping our society and economy. The Institute advocates a philosophy that adapts the progressive tradition in American politics to the realities of the Information Age and points to a "third way" beyond the liberal impulse to defend the bureaucratic status quo and the conservative bid to simply dismantle government. The Institute envisions government as society's servant, not its master—as a catalyst for a broader civic enterprise controlled by and responsive to the needs of citizens and the communities where they live and work.[6]

The formation of the Democratic Leadership Council originated in attempts to attract voters who crossed over to the Republican side during the backlash to antiwar demonstrations, Affirmative Action, forced integration of schools, welfare policies, and cultural-identity politics. These fleeing White middle-class voters, the New Democrats argued, no longer believed the Democratic party was working in their interests. In the 1960s and 1970s, according to New Democrats, the New Deal coalition crumbled as southern and northern working-class White voters concluded that the Democratic party represented the interests only of the poor, minority races, lesbians and gays, and pacifists.

The cofounders of the Progressive Policy Institute, Will Marshall and Robert Shapiro, were active in Democratic politics. Marshall worked for many Democratic senators and representatives and served as a staff member of the House Subcommittee on Government Efficiency. At the time of this writing, Marshall serves as both the project director of the Democratic Leadership Council and the president of the Progressive Policy Institute. While holding these positions, Marshall is a coeditor/author of the New Democratic manifesto, *Mandate for Change*, which formed the basic part of Clinton's 1992 political platform. Shapiro also worked in Congress and served as a contributing editor to *The New Republic*.[7]

Concerned with winning back White middle-class voters, the New Democrats eventually devised an educational platform that would give the middle class federal aid to attend college and programs for upgrading skills and finding new jobs.In 1990, the Progressive Policy Institute issued a strategy paper containing the ominous pronouncement: "It is time to say this: Our system of public education is a bad system. It is terribly inequitable. It does not meet the nation's needs and exploits teachers' altruism. It hurts kids."[8] Written by Ted Kolderie, a senior fellow of the Progressive Policy Institute, the policy paper advocated school choice and charter schools as solutions for the ills of public education. Kolderie argued that school choice was not meaningful unless parents and students were presented with real alternatives to the existing system. For Kolderie, this meant charter schools. As an alternative to a choice plan based on vouchers, Kolderie emphasized creating what he called "a new public school system" by allowing, "New schools … [to] be formed by educators—administrators or teachers—or by groups of parents. Other options include social-service agencies or private groups in the learning business."[9]

In response to pressure from the teacher unions, President Bill Clinton rejected the use of private groups in public education. Particularly distasteful to the unions was Kolderie's suggestion that they allow for-profit learning businesses to charter schools. Therefore, accepting the often-stated opinion that public schools needed "reinvention" for the Information Age, the New Democrats supported public school choice and public charter schools.

In 1996, the Democratic Leadership Council and the Progressive Policy Institute issued a key document in defining the New Democrats and its new educational policies: "The New Progressive Declaration: A Political Philosophy for the Information Age."[10] The document declares that the New Democrats must manage the transition to the new "Information Age," which requires an end to solving problems through "a larger, stronger central government" and "top-down paternalism."[11]

The Declaration offers three guiding principles for the Information Age. The first is enhancing equality of opportunity by breaking down the barriers to personal economic advancement by removing discriminatory barriers and "providing meaningful arenas for self-improvement."[12] Equality of opportunity, the Declaration states, "is the ideal of a society in which individuals earn their marks through their own talents and effort within a system of fair and open rules." Echoing this language, the "Improving Education" section of the 2004 Democratic Party Platform opens: "The simple bargain in the heart of the American Dream offers opportunity to every American who takes the responsibility to make the most of it."[13] In its "Five Strategies for Renewing Democracy," the New Progressive Declaration rejects redistributing wealth for "increasing opportunity through investing in economic growth and education."[14] And, of course, it is education that is supposed to ensure that all Americans have equality of opportunity. The Declaration announces a "Time of Radical Reform" that will create "an education system for the Information Age."[15]

Charter schools are specifically referred to in the Declaration's third guiding principle of achieving "genuine self-government" by empowering our citizens to act for themselves by decentralizing power, expanding individual choice, and injecting competition into the delivery of public goods and services."[16] It is important to note that the Declaration refers to competition in the "delivery of public goods and services" as opposed to the neoconservative stress on privatization. Public charter schools are cited as an example of competition between government agencies.

The New Democrats' educational program assumes that the plight of the modern worker in a global economy depends on rapidly changing job skills. This assumption results in an economic plan that leans heavily on education policies. For instance, consider the following problems and answers discussed by New Democrats:

1. Unemployment. The answer: educational opportunities to learn job skills needed in the new global economy.
2. Workers trapped in low-income and dead-end jobs. The answer: educational opportunities to improve job skills.
3. People who are unemployed because of restructuring and downsizing. The answer: educational opportunities to gain new job skills for the Information Age and global economy.
4. Increasing inequality in income and wealth. The answer: expanded educational opportunities for the middle class and poor.
5. Improved overall economy. The answer: reinventing U.S. public schools for the Information Age and educating workers and students in the skills needed to help the United States expand in the global economy.

There are two important and unproven assumptions to the New Democratic program. The first is that a skills mismatch between the worker and the labor market causes the basic problem of unemployment and dead-end jobs. Just give the worker the right skills, the New Democrats presume, and the problems are solved. This assumption, as I discuss, is currently being challenged. It is based on the relation between level of educational attainment and income. The problem in this assumption is educational inflation: As more people receive college degrees, the economic value of the college degree declines. In the context of educational inflation, the question is this: Can increased educational opportunities decrease economic inequalities?

THE DEMOCRATIC ROAD TO NO CHILD LEFT BEHIND:
BILL CLINTON AND THE NEW DEMOCRATS

The New Democratic commitment to the accountability, standards, charter schools provisions of No Child Left Behind can be traced back to President Bill Clinton's educational agenda when he was governor of Arkansas in the 1980s. After Bill Clinton lost the 1980 gubernatorial election, Hillary Clinton suggested that the next campaign should focus on education for economic revival. "Hillary Clinton," Meredith Oakley, the editor and political columnist of the *Arkansas-Democrat Gazette*, claimed, "was responsible for her husband's decision to emphasize education reform above all other matters."[17] This was 3 years before *A Nation at Risk* popularized the idea that educational reform was necessary to improve U.S. interests in global markets. During Clinton's successful 1982 gubernatorial election campaign he emphasized educational reform as the key to Arkansas's economic revival. Expansion of vocational and high-technology training programs, educational opportunity for the poor, and basic skills programs, Clinton claimed, would revitalize the state's economy.

After his second election, Clinton's campaign staff decided to create a public image of Clinton as the "education governor." The "education governor" image associated him with other southern governors using the same strategy. During the 1980s, Tennessee's Gov. Lamar Alexander—later the Senior President Bush's Secretary of Education—and South Carolina's Gov. Richard Riley—Clinton's future Secretary of Education—built their political careers on educational reform.

Hillary Clinton's role in designing Bill's educational image was extremely important. Beginning with her involvement as a lawyer in the Children's Defense Fund in the 1970s to the publication of her book, *It Takes a Village and Other Lessons Children Teach Us* (1996), she influenced the educational agenda of the New Democrats. One of the significant reform strategies she and Bill agreed on was the use of government-created academic standards. After Bill won the gubernatorial election in 1982, he worked for the passage of Arkansas's Quality Education Act of 1983 and promptly appointed Hillary to chair the Education Standards Committee, whose members agree that its final report reflected Hillary's agenda.[18]

As the reader already knows, the conviction that tough educational standards could reform schools haunted educational politics throughout the 1990s. Hillary's Education Standards Committee proposed the testing of third-, sixth-, and eighth-grade students and Arkansas's teachers. Bill Clinton accepted the recommendations and announced that he would not raise taxes to give teachers a salary increase until state teachers took a basic skills test. "No test, no tax," he told the public.[19]

Clinton's education platform improved his public image and his ratings in the polls.[20] His campaign strategists proclaimed that educational reform was a victory for the people and economy of Arkansas. In the public's mind, he was now the "education governor." With his popularity running high, Clinton spent little time campaigning in 1984. With the subsequent passage of legislation increasing the governor's term in office to 4 years, Clinton's position was secure.

Encouraged by the public image of "education governor," Clinton turned his attention to national politics. In 1986 he was elected vice chair-person of the National Governors Association. The chairperson of the organization was Lamar Alexander of Tennessee. In 1989, President Bush asked the National Governors' Association to develop what would become the Goals 2000 agenda. Embodied in Goals 2000 were the principles of testing and educational standards that were the backbone of Clinton's political career as governor of Arkansas.

Chairing the Democratic Leadership Council in 1991 and 1992, Clinton applied the lessons he learned in Arkansas to developing a strategy to win voters back to the Democratic Party. In 1991, Clinton voiced the concerns of the Democratic Leadership Council: "The working people and small-business people that used to vote for us don't anymore in a lot of tough elections because they have become convinced that the Democrats won't stand up for American interests abroad ... [and think we] will tax the middle class to give it to the poor with no strings attached."[21]

In 1992, the Democratic Leadership Council released programmatic guidelines in the form of *Mandate for Change* which was included in the Clinton and Gore 1992 campaign book *Putting People First: How We Can All Change America*. With the same spirit as that of antigovernment Republicans, Clinton and Gore declared in *Putting People First*: "We must take away power from the entrenched bureaucracies and special interests that dominate Washington."[22] The anti-big government stance of the New Democrats appeared in the 1996 Democratic national platform: "The American people do not want big government solutions."[23] By voicing an anti-big government attitude, New Democrats hope to distance themselves in the public mind from the frequently attacked image of liberals. During the 1996 campaign, when Bob Dole accused Clinton of being a closet liberal, Clinton lashed back, citing a record of reducing the deficit, supporting the death penalty, banning assault weapons, and reforming welfare as proof of his New Democratic centrist politics.[24]

The New Democratic anti-big government stance was tempered by a belief that government still has the important role of ensuring the fair provision of services, such as health care and education. Hillary Clinton maintained that government needs to be trimmed but that it should not be made ineffectual in "fulfilling its basic responsibilities: (1) to build a strong, globally competitive economy that grows the middle class and shrinks the underclass; (2) to bring Americans together ... to fulfill their obligations to families, the environment, and those who need and deserve support."[25] Responding to radical antigovernment Austrian economists, Hillary Clinton warned that their rhetoric "argues against the excesses of government but not against excesses of the marketplace."[26] She wondered who would benefit from the elimination of government regulations controlling water pollution and whether the pursuit of profit in a free market would solve the problem.

Casting suspicion on proponents of marketplace economics and radical limitation of government activities, Hillary Clinton insisted that "this perspective exalts private initiative and regards those who exercise it as deserving to flourish virtually unencumbered by any mandate to share the wealth or apply it toward solving our common problems and creating common opportunities."[27]

In the 1996 campaign book *Between Hope and History: Meeting America's Challenges for the 21st Century*, Bill Clinton complained that the American political debate was divided between those arguing "for the government to spend more money on the same bureaucracies working in the same way" and those arguing "that government is inherently bad and all our problems would be solved if ... government [got] out of the way."[28] Clinton responded to these differences by indicating that between 1980 and 1992, when antigovernment attitudes dominated political rhetoric, the United States had the slowest job growth since the Depression, its national debt quadrupled, and society became more racially and ethnically divided. The "reinvented" government of the New Democrats will supposedly solve these problems.[29]

Consequently, New Democrats proposed that federal and state governments should "create a set of national standards for what students should know" while trusting the competition of the market to reinvent the school. In this context the federal government would act as a big sister or brother, helping states to carry out national mandates. For example, in *Putting People First*, Clinton and Gore argued that schools would be reformed by helping "states develop public school choice programs like those of Arkansas with protection from discrimination based on race, religion, or income."[30]

To attract middle-class voters, New Democrats shifted their focus from using education to help the poor achieve equality of opportunity to aiding middle-class families struggling to send their children to college. Rather than referring to the war on poverty, New Democrats use the term *lifetime learning*. The promise of lifetime learning is equal educational opportunity for all age groups and social classes. In *Putting People First* Clinton and Gore described their lifetime-learning strategy as investing "in our people at every stage of their lives."[31] They claimed that the strategy would put people first by dramatically improving the way parents prepared their children for school, giving students the chance to train for jobs or pay for college, and providing workers with the training and retraining they needed to compete and win in tomorrow's economy. Clinton's 1996 campaign promises dramatically illustrate the New Democrats' desire to extend government educational benefits to the middle class and to support lifetime learning. At the 1996 Democratic convention Clinton declared his intention to "make two years of college just as universal ... as a high school education is today."[32] To achieve this goal, he proposed a $1,500-a-year tuition tax credit that he described as "a hope scholarship for the first two years of college to make the typical community college education available to every American."[33] In addition, he called for a $10,000 income tax deduction for college tuition for working families and a $2,600 instructional grant to underemployed or unemployed workers for job training. In words highlighting the New Democrats' attempted appeal to the middle class, Clinton told convention delegates and television viewers, "We should not tax middle-income Americans for the money they spend on college. We'll get the money back down the road many times over."[34]

In *Between Hope and History* Clinton echoed his Secretary of Labor Robert Reich's analysis of labor market problems: "There are people," Clinton observed, "principally the bottom half of America's hourly wage earners, who are working hard but aren't getting ahead because they don't have the kind of skills that are rewarded in this global economy."[35] Expressing concern about the splintering of the middle class as corporate restructuring forces many into the "anxious class" who must worry about debt and the next job, Hillary Clinton concluded that "midlevel managers and white-collar workers are increasingly vulnerable to becoming what Secretary of Labor Robert Reich calls 'frayed-collar workers in gold-plated times.'"[36]

Appealing to the anxious class of middle- and working-class voters, the New Democrats offer broadened educational opportunities as solutions to the problems of declining real incomes, corporate restructuring and downsizing, and job insecurity. A fundamental premise of New Democrats—including the Clintons, Reich, and John Kerry—is that U.S. wages and jobs will not be protected from competition with the global labor market. Unlike laborers in the past, U.S. workers cannot feel secure in the knowledge that their wages are higher than those of workers in other countries doing comparable work. In the language of New Democrats, "competitive worker" refers to competition in a global market. Ultimately, this could mean a U.S. textile worker receiving the same wage as a textile worker in India or Honduras. In this context, if U.S. workers are going to achieve high salaries, then they must be trained for jobs that receive a high income in world labor markets.

Reich was the economic sage of the New Democrats. Important reasons for his influence are his 1991 book, *The Work of Nations: Preparing Ourselves for*

21st-Century Capitalism; his experience as an advisor in the Ford and Carter administrations; and his contributing editorship of *The New Republic*. Reich was a major influence on the Clinton administration's policies for education and human capital. He concluded that there was a close connection between competitiveness in the global economy, education, and income. The global labor market, not a limited national labor market, determined the salaries of U.S. workers. All laborers must now compete in a global economy, according to Reich: "Some Americans, whose contributions to the global economy are more highly valued in world markets, will succeed, while others, whose contributions are deemed far less valuable, fail .... Some Americans may command much higher rewards; others, far lower."[37]

Therefore, according to Reich's analysis, raising income levels and overcoming the insecurities of the anxious class requires training people for jobs that are highly rewarded in the global economy. This means changing the education of the entire American workforce. In a global market, "routine production services" are no longer as economically rewarding to American workers as they were in past labor markets. Americans who work in routine production services, which include traditional blue-collar manufacturing, new technology production lines, and data clerks, now compete for wages with workers in Asia, Mexico, Central and South America, and other areas. Consequently, American routine-production workers will either lose their jobs or receive lower wages as multinational corporations search the globe for cheap labor supplies. What Reich described as "in-person services" are dead-end jobs with low pay and no future. In-person services include the jobs of fast-food employees, janitors, cashiers, hospital attendants and orderlies, and others who provide a direct service. As Reich noted, these jobs require little more than a grade school education and some vocational training. Many workers who are displaced from routine-production jobs find themselves sliding down the wage scale to in-person services.

The top income on Reich's symbolic job list goes to "symbolic-analytical service," which requires a high level of education in the manipulation of symbols—data, visual, oral, and written—and includes the work of research scientists; engineers; public relations experts; investment bankers; real estate developers; accountants; and a whole list of consultants, specialists, managers, and media experts. These are the jobs, according Reich, that command the largest salaries in the global marketplace.

Therefore, within Reich's framework, the ideal economic plan increases incomes for American workers and makes them competitive for global jobs by improving education and training so that workers can compete as symbolic analysts. In addition, Reich contended, this strategy will prevent the increasing inequalities in wealth and income in the United States. In a chapter entitled, "Why the Rich Are Getting Richer and the Poor, Poorer," Reich asserted that "the fortunes of routine producers are declining. In-person servers are also becoming poorer, although their fates are less clear-cut. But symbolic analysts—who solve, identify, and broker new problems—are, by and large, succeeding in the world economy."[38]

Reich admitted that important obstacles may hinder the ability of education to make American workers more competitive. One problem is the tendency for symbolic analysts to protect the educational advantages of their children by living in protected suburban communities with good schools or by sending their children to private schools. In the global economy, educational advantages become a new form of inheritance passed on from generation to generation. Educational inheritance creates a cycle of well-educated families sending their children to good schools to become well educated so they can continue to pass on educational benefits to their children.

In this cycle of educational inheritance, the symbolic-analyst class displays little concern for the education of other people's children, particularly those of middle- and low-income working families and the poor. Reich contended that global corporations no longer have a commitment to support the infrastructure of any particular nation. As corporations hop around the globe looking for workers and consumers, the allegiance of the highest paid employees—symbolic analysts—is to their own families and social class. Why should symbolic analysts in India worry about the educational conditions of the Indian masses? Symbolic analysts are mainly concerned with finding top-quality schools for their children. In fact, an overeducated workforce could lead to demands from routine production workers for higher wages or to social unrest.[39]

Shirking their own responsibilities, corporations, according to Reich, demand tax breaks while giving lip service to supporting quality public schools. For example, Reich wrote, "The executives of General Motors, ... who have been among the loudest to proclaim the need for better schools, have also been among the most relentless pursuers of local tax abatements." Reich cited the example of Tarrytown, New York, where a tax break for General Motors resulted in the laying off of schoolteachers.[40]

Consequently, Reich said he hoped corporations will return to an era of corporate responsibility by ensuring quality public schools for all, improving social conditions, and supporting the welfare of their workers. In the global economy, Reich maintained, corporations have lost all sense of corporate responsibility. Corporations move into communities demanding tax breaks that ultimately mean cuts in local school budgets. Corporations abandon communities, leaving behind a crumbling school system and infrastructure. Corporations now downsize and restructure while showing little concern for the welfare of employees and their families. Why should symbolic analysts worry about crumbling communities, abandoned workers, and decaying school systems if they can find a protected suburb of like-minded people and good schools for their children?[41]

The economic program of the New Democrats includes improving corporate responsibility and educational opportunities. In *Between Hope and History*, Clinton praised the efforts of the Xerox Corporation for its support of the Urban Family Institute in Washington, DC, which tries to improve the educational futures for at-risk children by providing counseling and emotional support.[42] Clinton proudly recalled the words of Gerald Greenwald, CEO of United Airlines, at a conference on corporate citizenship the administration organized: "Every CEO in America says employees are our most important asset. Well, if that's true, why do we invest more in the overhaul of our machinery than we do in the training ... of our employees?"[43]

Hillary Clinton was encouraged by the words of Harvard Business School Professor Michael Porter: "Companies will understand the need to rebuild the corporation and create a sense of community again. The ones that do that will be winners in the next stage of competition."[44] She cited examples of corporate responsibility involving a Cleveland supermarket chain that renovated stores in depressed neighborhoods; an Illinois automotive manufacturer who set aside acres of play space for employee families and provided family-friendly benefits, such as college scholarships, a daycare center, and subsidized tutoring; and a bus company that hired and trained workers who were previously considered unemployable.[45]

The 1996 Democratic national platform emphatically supported the idea of corporations assuming responsibility for the infrastructure of their communities and the welfare of their workers. Under the heading "Corporate Citizenship," the platform stated:

> Employers have a responsibility to do their part as well .... The Democratic Party insists that corporate leaders invest in the long-term, by providing workers with living wages and benefits, education and training, a safe, healthy place to work, and opportunities for greater involvement in company decision making and ownership. Employers must make sure workers share in the benefits of the good years.[46]

Policies for increasing educational opportunities and gaining corporate commitment are an extension of Clinton's politically successful education policies in Arkansas and his work on Goals 2000. Referring to Bush's education summit and Goals 2000, Clinton gave this reminder to readers of his 1996 campaign book: "In 1989, I and the rest of the nation's governors ... were convinced that the more you expect of students, the more they expect of themselves and more they achieve."[47] World-class standards and tests, according to this argument, will increase student achievement and help American workers compete in the global labor market.

Signed by Clinton in 1994, the Goals 2000: Educate America Act and the School-to-Work Act embodied the educational hopes of New Democrats. At the signing of the School-to-Work Act Reich declared, "There should not be a barrier between education and work. We're talking about a new economy in which lifelong learning is a necessity for every single member of the American workforce."[48]

In supporting the Goals 2000: Educate America Act, New Democrats emphasize the unproven assumption that increasing educational standards will improve the schooling of American workers and, consequently, increase wages and decrease economic inequalities. Marshall Smith, speaking at a Brookings Institute conference on national standards 2 months after the signing of the legislation, opened his speech with these remarks:

> The need for American students to learn more demanding content and skills became increasingly clear in the 1980s. The United States faces great challenges: internally, by the need to maintain a strong democracy in a complex and diverse society; externally, by a competitive economic environment that will be dominated by high-skills jobs.[49]

Marshall repeated the unproven maxim of the standards movement that children will learn more if they are challenged by high standards. Concerning Clinton's Goals 2000 legislation, Marshall contended that high academic standards will result in high academic achievement for all students because "it builds on our understanding that all children can learn to higher levels than we have previously thought."[50]

An important assumption of New Democratic strategy is that all students will have equal access to the teachers, books, educational materials, and laboratories required to meet national or state academic standards. The children of symbolic analysts in privileged public or private schools certainly have the opportunity to achieve these standards. Yet what about students attending schools in impoverished rural and urban areas where there is a shortage of textbooks, learning materials, science laboratories, and quality teachers?

Faced with these questions, the New Democrats backtracked to liberal programs of the 1960s and the war on poverty. The 1994 reauthorization of the 1965 Elementary and Secondary Education Act (ESEA), which targeted the problems of "disadvantaged" (a 1960s euphemism for poverty-level) students, was given the hopeful title of the Improving America's Schools Act. According to New Democrats, it was this type of program, with its benefits primarily going to the poor, that drove low- and middle-income voters from the Democratic party. Although focused on helping the same poor population, New Democrats tried to change the legislation's public image by this assertion: "The difference in this reauthorization is that the focus is enhanced opportunities for these students to learn to the same challenging standards as other, more advantaged students."[51]

The Goals 2000: Educate America Act contained a provision to bridge the obvious gap between national and state standards and the "savage inequalities" in the American school system. The Goals 2000 legislation introduced opportunity-to-learn (OTL) standards as "the criteria for … assessing … [the ability] of the education system … to provide all students with an opportunity to learn the material in voluntary national content standards or state content standards."[52] Besides providing for a new area of growth for bureaucrats and educational experts as they tried to achieve "scientific" measurements of school inequalities, the OTL standards held out the hope of finally addressing the issue of inequalities in educational opportunity. In the past, neoconservatives and New Democrats skillfully avoided the politically charged issue of equal funding of school systems. Currently, state court systems are considering legal suits against inequitable school funding. Upper and middle-class suburbanites are unwilling to give up their educational advantages, and they are resistant to being taxed to upgrade poorer school districts. As Reich asserted, symbolic analysts are mainly interested in protecting the educational advantages of their children.[53]

The OTL standards were to remedy the inequality problems posed by national and state tests. According to Andrew Porter of the Wisconsin Center for Education Research, one of the federal government's experts hired to make scientific sense of the standard, "The initial motivation for OTL standards stems from an equity concern that high-stakes assessments of student achievement are fair only if students have had an adequate opportunity to learn the content assessed in those high-stakes tests."[54]

As one might have predicted, OTL standards did not fare well in the 1994 Congress, during which Republicans vowed to end federal involvement in education and eliminate the Department of Education. This left New Democrat Bill Clinton with only liberal programs, such as ESEA and Head Start, to remedy the most obvious flaw in Goals 2000.

Clinton, therefore, avoided commenting during the 1996 campaign about inequalities in educational opportunity and the educational needs of America's poorest children. Echoing the first goal of Goals 2000, "All children in America will start school ready to learn," Clinton offered the voters expanded funding of Head Start, a liberal and popular program of the 1960s that prepares children from poor families to enter school. Hillary Clinton could offer examples of successful educational projects only for low-income school districts, such as Reading Recovery, the Efficacy Institute, James Comer's family schools, and Education Excellence for Children (EEXCEL). These limited programs with limited funding are hardly answers to the savage inequalities in U.S. schools.

Consequently, the 1996 Democratic campaign focused on making American workers more competitive by expanding college opportunities. "Higher education," the 1996 Democratic national platform proclaimed, "is the key to a successful future in the 21st century. The typical worker with a college education earns 73% more than one without."[55] This approach offered benefits to middle- and lower income families and avoided the difficult issues of poverty and inequality. Workers' skills were to be upgraded, and Reich's dreams fulfilled, by a combination of tuition tax credits for the first 2 college years, tax deductions for all education after high school, a new GI bill granting $2,600 in tuition grants to unemployed workers, and the continuation of previous Clinton-backed educational legislation providing increased student loans and Pell grants and an opportunity for students to work their way through college by doing community work in Americorps.[56]

REINVENTING GOVERNMENT AND SCHOOLS: THE DEMOCRATIC ROAD TO NO CHILD LEFT BEHIND

The idea of reinventing government and schools is key to understanding New Democrats and their support of the accountability, standards, and charter schools provisions of No Child Left Behind. According to political writer Jacob Weisberg, "The most influential New Democratic idea—and perhaps the only widely read New Democratic book—is *Reinventing Government*."[57] Without adopting an antigovernment stance, David Osborne and Ted Gaebler's *Reinventing Government: How the Entrepreneurial Spirit Is Transforming the Public Sector* gives New Democrats a plan for erasing the Democratic image of being boosters of big government.[58] The essence of the anti-big government solutions offered in Reinventing Government is captured in the following 1996 Democratic national platform declaration: "today's Democratic Party believes in a government that works better and costs less .... We are committed to reinventing government .... The American people do not want big government solutions .... They want a government that ... enhances their quality of life."[59]

Similar to the many tracts by neoconservatives, *Reinventing Government* is a product of the New Democratic think tank, the Progressive Policy Institute. The lead author, David Osborne, is a senior fellow at the institute and served as senior advisor to Gore's National Performance Review, which attempted to reform the federal government. After the publication of *Reinventing Government*, Osborne founded the Reinventing Government Network and the Alliance for Redesigning Government. Osborne's coauthor, Ted Gaebler, is a former city manager.[60]

The basic thesis of *Reinventing Government* is that "the kind of government that developed during the industrial era, with their sluggish, centralized bureaucracies, their preoccupations with rules and regulations, and their hierarchical chains of command, no longer work very well."[61] If the authors had substituted schools for government, their thesis would have sounded exactly like the warning about obsolescent schools in the 1983 educational report *A*

Nation at Risk. On the basis of their discussion of this thesis, Osborne and Gaebler offered suggestions for reinventing government and public schools. Their ideas can be boiled down to seven basic principles:

1. Competition should be created between service providers. For education, this means creating competition between public schools through a choice plan.
2. Citizens should be empowered by transferring control from government bureaucracies to the community. For schools, this means creating for each public school site-based management teams or governance boards consisting of parents, teachers, community members, and school administrators.
3. Outputs rather than inputs should be used to measure government performance. For education, this means rewarding students, teachers, and schools with merit pay for successful grades or student achievement.
4. Missions, not rules and regulations, should guide government agencies. For education, this means being guided by the mission of attaining Goals 2000.
5. Government agencies should consider citizens as customers. For schools, this means choice.
6. Government should anticipate and prepare for future problems. Although there is no direct discussion of education in this category of government reform, I could imagine educational planners thinking about any potential issues in the education of first graders that might affect these students in high school.
7. Government should be decentralized by replacing hierarchical control with teamwork. For school systems, this means the shifting of decision-making power from a school district's central bureaucracy to a site-based management team at the school level.

In the "Reinventing Public Education" section of their final chapter, Osborne and Gaebler stressed the importance of school choice, decentralizing authority, and creating "a system of accountability that focuses on results, rather than compliance on rules and regulations."[62] In this context, state governments and local school boards would set minimum educational standards, enforce social equity, and arrange financing of schools. Osborne and Gaebler suggested, "But the school districts would not operate public schools. Public schools would be run—on something like a contract or voucher basis—by many different organizations: teachers, colleges, even community organizations."[63] Furthermore, they argued, public schools should be encouraged to earn extra tax money by attracting more students in the competitive market created by school choice.

In the spirit of reinvention, the 1996 Democratic national platform called for an expansion of public school choice and the promotion of public charter schools.[64] In harmony with reinventing schools and government, the platform promised to reduce federal regulations and to "give local schools, teachers, and principals the flexibility they need to meet [Goals 2000] standards."[65] Also, Hillary Clinton supported public school choice and public charter schools.[66] In contrast to the Republican party, the Democratic party stresses that reinvention of school by choice and charters should be limited to public schools. In part, this shows the New Democratic commitment to retaining public control of tax monies. The New Democrats are unwilling to turn public school money over to privately controlled institutions. Their stance also highlights the power of the two teachers' unions. Since the 1970s, the two teachers' unions, with their rich coffers and large memberships, have remained loyal to the Democratic party. These two unions vehemently oppose any choice plan that includes private schools. Currently, the existence of the two unions depends on the continuation of the present public school system. For the same reason, the two teachers' unions oppose privately controlled charter schools, particularly for-profit schools.

Exhibiting the idealism and self-interest of New Democrats and the teachers' unions, the 1996 Democratic national platform urged that tax dollars "should not be taken from public schools and give[n] ... to private schools" and that public charter schools should be "held to the highest standards of accountability and access."[67]

During the first televised Presidential debate on October 6, 1996, Clinton slightly modified his stand on limiting choice to public schools by suggesting that states and local communities could create private school choice plans. However, he felt that this would take money away from public schools. With the ambiguous rhetoric that characterizes political campaigns, Clinton made this statement during the debate:

> I support school choice .... But if you're going to have a private voucher plan, that ought to be determined by states and localities where they're raising and spending most of the money. I simply think it's wrong to take money away from programs that are helping build basic skills for kids—90% of them are in the public schools—to take money away from programs that are helping fund the school lunch program, that are helping to fund the other programs, that are helping schools to improve their standards.[68]

In campaign speeches, Clinton clearly linked charter schools to teacher power and public accountability. After announcing a $1.3 million federal grant for California charter schools, Clinton explained his conception of charter schools at a rally in Rancho Cucamonga on September 12: "[A charter school is] where a group of teachers get together and say 'here's who we're going to serve; here's what we're going to produce; give us a charter and if we don't produce it, take it away from us; hold us accountable."[69]

THE DEMOCRATIC ROAD TO NO CHILD LEFT BEHIND:
AL GORE AND THE 2000 PRESIDENTIAL CAMPAIGN

During the 2000 Presidential campaign, Al Gore reiterated the New Democratic vision of public schools preparing workers for the global economy. His published educational agenda linked his positions to those of the Clinton administration. "[Gore]," the 2000 educational agenda stated, "will build on and extend the aggressive efforts since 1993 to improve our schools through higher standards, extra help to students who need it the most, and equal access to higher education."[70] Also, reflecting the human capital arguments of the New Democrats, the 2000 national Democratic platform titled its section on education "Investing in Americans."[71] The stamp of the New Democratic ideology on the purposes of education opened this section of the platform: "Democrats know that today, more than ever before, we need the right kinds of investments—in education, lifelong learning, skill development, and research and development—to take advantage of the vast opportunities of the Information Age."[72]

The major changes in Al Gore's 2000 educational agenda, as compared to Clinton's 1992 campaign, were calls for a more expanded role for public schooling and a more detailed approach to changing public schools. The Gore agenda called for the expansion of preschool programs, the creation of second-chance schools for students with serious problems, increased afterschool care, expanded summer school for failing students, and the reformation of failing schools. The last item, the reformation of failing public schools, eventually found its way into No Child Left Behind. The Gore agenda also suggested that public schools could be improved with the training of better teachers, creating smaller classrooms and schools, and the empowering of principals to hire their own staff and manage their schools' budgets.

During Gore's campaign, the Progressive Policy Institute announced on June 29, 2000 the creation of the "21st Century Schools Project" with the goal of developing "education policy and foster[ing] innovation to ensure that America's public schools are an engine of equal opportunity in the knowledge economy."[73] The project promised to improve accountability, equal access to education, teacher quality, and to "expand choice and innovation within public education." Reiterating a favorite theme among New Democrats that the basic nature of the economy had changed, the Project announced:

> American schools are based on an industrial-era model matched to an economy that is disappearing. The information-based economy requires greater skills and knowledge and demands that students reach higher levels of educa-

tion. This means that systemic change at all levels of education is required to move from a factory model public monopoly to a public education system premised on standards, choice, and publicly accountable schools.[74]

After Gore's defeat, the Project's emphasis on standards, choice, and accountability would parallel efforts by the Congressional New Democratic Coalition to create a comprehensive school reform plan which would eventually become part of No Child Left Behind. Listed as a key principle of the Project's work was: "Governments must at once demand more from our public schools through meaningful standards and accountability for results, and also must support greater innovation and diversity among schools through choice and competition."[75]

NEW DEMOCRATS' SUPPORT OF NO CHILD LEFT BEHIND: DID GEORGE W. BUSH STEAL THEIR AGENDA?

The New Democrats were quick to claim credit for the passage of No Child Left Behind and claim that President George W. Bush had stolen their ideas. On December 12, 2001, shortly before passage of the legislation, the Progressive Policy Institute issued a press release titled: "Education Reform Legislation Reflects Policy Ideas Proposed by PPI." The press release announced, "PPI is pleased that the education bill congress is poised to pass adopts a Third Way approach based on PPI ideas, to go beyond tired left–right debates on education and refocus federal education policy on improving achievement and equity for all children …. Although "No Child Left Behind" does not include every reform proposed by PPI, it is an excellent down payment on sustained reform and reflects the key PPI priorities of **accountability, flexibility, targeting and investment, and public school choice.**"[76]

On December 13, 2001, the New Democratic Coalition issued a press release announcing, "Leaders of the New Democrat Coalition (NDC), a prominent group of 74 centrist, pro-growth Democratic members of the House of Representatives, hailed the education bill given final approval by the House today for its consensus approach to reforming our schools and noted its similarities to their own education plan …. New Democrats today supported passage of the bipartisan No Child Left Behind Act conference report."[77]

"How Bush Stole Education" by Andrew J. Rotherham was published in the March 25, 2001 Democratic Leadership Council's *Blueprint Magazine*. Rotherham wrote, "When it was pointed out that Mr. Bush was appropriating many New Democratic education ideas, the Bush team cited it as evidence of their candidate's moderate credentials."[78] Rotherham went on to claim, "Mr. Bush's education agenda is largely a New Democratic one …. The new education bill, which is regarded widely as 'Bush's education initiative,' was largely written by Democratic Sens. Joe Lieberman (Conn.) and Evan Bayh (Ind.) along with other New Democrats."[79] Bemoaning the fact that No Child Left Behind was associated with President Bush and not the New Democrats, Rotherham asserted, "The president's coup undermines Democrats in crucial 2002 elections by perpetuating, to the delight of Republicans, a debilitating view of the Democratic Party as a tool of the teachers' unions."[80]

So what ideas did the New Democrats claim Bush and the Republicans had stolen? The Progressive Policy Institute claimed the ideas of holding schools, districts, and states accountable for achieving educational proficiency and "establishing school report cards to hold schools, districts and states accountable to parents and the public."[81] The New Democrats argued that Bush stole the idea that school districts and states should be required to improve failing schools; this had been part of Al Gore's agenda during the 2000 election. Also, the Institute claimed the ideas of "giving children in failing schools the right to transfer to another public school" and support of public charter schools. The Institute's press release on No Child Left Behind states:

> PPI has been at the forefront of advancing the charter school concept to improve public education, spur innovation, expand parental choice and move our schools from a factory model public monopoly to a public education system premised on standards, choice and publicly accountable schools. Public school choice and charter schools give parents options and provide alternatives for students trapped in low-performing schools, while also preserving accountability.[82]

The New Democratic Coalition claimed responsibility for those parts of the legislation dealing with accountability, aid to low performing schools, and public school choice. The Council listed the following as New Democratic ideas in No Child Left Behind:

Increased Accountability and Focus on Results

- Establishes a comprehensive accountability system that requires schools and school districts to show results for all students, and annual progress for low-performing racial and ethnic groups.
- Stronger professional development standards and training for teachers.
- Required state and school district report cards.
- Increased commitment to public school choice.[83]

If the New Democrats claimed the accountability, aid to low-performing schools, state school report cards, and charter schools of No Child Left Behind, then what were the exclusively Republican sections of the legislation? If the New Democrats were accurate about their contributions to the legislation, then Republican contributions were privatization of school services, the use of faith-based organizations, phonics-based reading instruction, school prayer, English acquisition, traditional American history, and Boy Scout access to public schools.

Did all Republicans *really* approve of No Child Left Behind and its massive federal intrusion into public schools? Rotherham claims, "They [Republicans] grudgingly acquiesced to the education bill only because it was a top White House priority. Rep. Tom DeLay (R–Texas) confessed to Rush Limbaugh that he 'voted for that awful education bill' only to support President Bush. "I came here to eliminate the Department of Education so it was very hard for me to vote for something that expands [it]."[84]

NO CHILD LEFT BEHIND, JOHN KERRY, AND THE 2004 PRESIDENTIAL CAMPAIGN

During the 2004 presidential campaign, John Kerry ignored the storm of protest from parents and educators that No Child Left Behind's accountability provisions were causing teachers to "teach to the test," resulting in increasing rigidity of classroom practices. Kerry's major complaint was that the Bush administration had not fully funded the legislation. Immediately before and after the passage of No Child Left Behind, the publishing market was literally flooded with books criticizing standards and standardized testing. Book titles expressed outrage about standards, tests, and corporate criticism of schools, such as *One Size Fits Few: The Folly of Educational Standards* by Susan Ohanian and Kathy Emery; *The Case Against Standardized Testing: Raising the Scores, Ruining the Schools* by Alfie Kohn; *Standardized Minds: The High Price of America's Testing Culture and What We Can Do to Change It* by Peter Sacks; and *Why Is Corporate America Bashing Our Schools?* by Susan Ohanian.[85]

Prominent among attempts by educators to wean Democratic Candidate John Kerry away from support of No Child Left Behind was University of Arizona Professor Ken Goodman, a pioneer of whole language reading instruction. He created a website, www.sosvoice.org, dedicated to repeal of No Child Left Behind which instructed viewers: "If you agree that Kerry and Edwards should take a stronger stand against NCLB and support the parents, teachers, and students who are being hurt by this punitive law call Kerry's office and tell them that. Share your personal stories with them of the harm being done to schools, teachers, kids and parents. Together we can make a difference."[86] Viewers of Goodman's Web site voted 75.5% to repeal the legislation, 18.4% to rewrite it, and 6.1% that it couldn't work.

Goodman posted "Ten Alarming Facts About No Child Left Behind." If his facts were true, they indicated that New Democrats and neoconservatives had not considered the potential impact of their elaborate federal accountability system. Among Goodman's most serious charges is that the legislation is forcing teachers and students out of schools, and forcing public schools to submit to a national curriculum and nationalized teaching methods. Goodman claims the following in his "Ten Alarming Facts":

1. The long- and short-term effects of NCLB will be devastating for American education ... The ultimate goal is to privatize American education ....

2. Within a neoconservative movement to privatize all aspects of American society, a heavily funded and well-organized campaign has created NCLB to discredit and destroy public education ....

3. NCLB is driving both students and teachers out of education. There is already a dramatic increase in dropouts and pushouts from high schools due to increased high-stakes testing, the narrowing of curriculum, and controls on how and what teachers may teach .... Many highly professional teachers are leaving teaching or taking early retirement to escape being required to conform to aspects of the law that they believe make it impossible to teach in the best interests of their pupils ....

4. NCLB centralizes control of every aspect of American education, including policy, methodology, curriculum, choice of text books, evaluation, and staffing, shifting power from local districts and states to a Washington bureaucracy. NCLB establishes a national curriculum and methodology in reading and mathematics and other fields ....

5. NCLB defines what is and isn't science. Through a series of panels, laws, and mandates, the federal government has defined what is science so narrowly, that 95 percent of scientific study in education has been swept aside as unscientific and decades of research has been wiped off federal websites such as ERIC ....

6. NCLB makes scores on mandatory tests the basis of all major decision-making in the schools, including which schools are failing ....

7. The law requires busing of pupils, at district expense, from non-improved schools to other schools .... Even Mayor Daley in Chicago is complaining about moving hundreds of kids from failing school to failing school.

8. NCLB controls who may teach and not teach and how they will be certified. Federal standards are established which take control away from states in the name of assuring qualified teachers in every class ....

9. Enforcement of NCLB employs blacklists. A list of who and what conforms and does not conform to NCLB criteria is being used to blacklist people, institutions, methods, and materials ....

10. NCLB, the federal law, is unconstitutional, as it violates the Constitution, which leaves education to the states. NCLB affects every

child and teacher in every school in the United States. It establishes a national curriculum and methodology in reading and math.[87]

Kerry and his Vice Presidential running mate John Edwards ignored complaints about testing and failed to criticize the Republican agenda in No Child Left Behind such as school prayer, privatization, and Boy Scouts. In their campaign book, *Our Plan for America: Stronger At Home, Respected in the World*, they stated, "We both voted for that landmark legislation, which created a new bargain with states and school districts: we will ask more from you, and we will make sure you have the resources to get the job done. The Bush administration has broken that promise; we will keep it."[88] In *A Call to Service*, Kerry stated that his efforts at school reform in the 1990s reflected the Democratic centrist position. This led to his support of No Child Left Behind: "I later introduced my own comprehensive education reform bill in the Senate. Then, when momentum built behind a similar, bipartisan proposal, I sponsored an effort for change. In 2001 President Bush endorsed what had been a *centrist Democratic bill*; the result was No Child Left Behind Act [emphasis added]."[89] The 2004 Democratic Platform addressed complaints about standardized testing with the short statement: "We will use testing to advance real learning, not undermine it, by developing high-quality assessments that measure the complex skills students need to develop."[90]

In *A Call to Service*, Kerry frames his educational policies in the Clinton rhetoric of competition for jobs in a global labor market. In addition, he stresses that education involves the development of human capital for economic growth. In Democratic centrist language, he asserts, "We are the nation furthest advanced toward an information-age economy in which the knowledge and skills of our people are our most important labor and capital assets. We know that we need a rapidly expanding workforce of well-educated and well-trained individuals; they're more important to our economy than all our oil, minerals, or timber."[91] In reference to the goal of having Americans occupy the highest paid jobs in the global economy, Kerry proclaims, "And we also know that the longstanding American aspirations of equal opportunity and upward mobility depend on an educational system that equips our people—all of our people—to occupy the high-wage jobs that brainpower can command."[92]

Reflecting Kerry and the New Democratic theme that education was key to making American workers more competitive in a globalized labor market, the 2004 Democratic Platform stressed education in science and math, and making higher education affordable for all Americans. The 2004 Democratic Platform proposed making higher education more accessible by ensuring that student aid be made more simple and provided faster; and offering "generous" tax credits "to reduce the price of four years of college for all students."[93] Restating the Democratic theme since the Clinton years, the Platform asserted, "At a time when all good jobs increasingly depend on advanced skills, we will strengthen technical training for those who do not attend college. Finally, we must place a special emphasis on expanding achievement in math and science. These are subjects where America has always led the world and must continue to lead in the 21st century."[94]

The importance of distance learning and community colleges for increasing and improving the quality of American jobs was stressed in the 2004 Democratic Platform's section: "A Strong, Growing Economy: Creating Good Jobs." In this section the Platform declared, "We will make sure that Americans are the best-skilled, best-trained workers in the world. In addition to reforming K-12 education, we will expand training and opportunities for Americans of all ages." Regarding job training, the Platform promised, "We will support regional skills alliances, workforce development conducted at community colleges, and other initiatives that prepare workers for high-skills jobs that offer family-sustaining wages and benefits. And we will support high-quality distance learning so that Americans everywhere can use a keyboard to learn from experts anywhere."[95]

Ironically, given the expanded educational bureaucracy at federal and state levels to create and monitor the standards and testing requirements of No Child Left Behind, Kerry used the anti-bureaucratic language to support his educational platform: "First, we need to place more emphasis on teaching and less on bureaucracy. Look at most school boards in this country and you will see a classic industrial-age bureaucracy seeking to own and operate every aspect of public education and to micromanage the activities of everyone working in the schools."[96] Similar to neoconservatives who envision a free market for education with government regulation through standards and tests, Kerry advocated letting local schools develop their own innovative methods for meeting accountability standards. In reality, as suggested before, this simply shifts local bureaucratic control to state and federal levels. Kerry proclaimed, "We need to give public institutions more freedom from micromanagement in exchange for strict accountability for achieving tangible improvements in the knowledge and skills of our children."[97]

Similar to President Clinton and other New Democrats, Kerry supported public charter schools as part of the reinventing of educational governance. Referring to the Community Day Charter School in Lawrence, Massachusetts, Kerry claimed, "You have to observe a good charter school in action to appreciate the revolutionary nature of what too often sounds like an academic concept."[98] He reported that two thirds of the Massachusetts public charter schools had the best state test scores in their school districts. Kerry rejected attempts to privatize school choice through a voucher system that allows parental choice of private schools:

"Many have argued for reform through the public financing of vouchers for private schools, but I believe this is pushing the country in the wrong direction. Vouchers allocate resources not among competing public schools but out of the system entirely."[99]

Since the two teachers unions—the National Education Association and the American Federation of Teachers—give strong support to the Democratic Party, it is not surprising that the John Kerry and the 2004 Democratic Party platform class advocated increased pay for teachers. To put a great teacher in every classroom, the Democratic Platform proposed, "We must raise pay for teachers, especially in the schools and subjects where great teachers are in the shortest supply." And carrying accountability to the next level, the Platform approved testing of teachers. And, in response to criticism that the teachers unions have made it difficult to remove ineffective teachers, and at the same time avoiding offending the teachers unions, the Platform avowed, "And teachers deserve due process protection from arbitrary dismissal, but we must have fast, fair procedures for improving or removing teachers who do not perform on the job."[100]

Approved in July 2004, themes in the Democratic Platform continued to be elaborated by the Progressive Policy Institute's "21st Century Schools Project," which started during Al Gore's 2000 presidential campaign. In September 2004, the Progressive Policy Institute issued its "National Strategy to Expand Early Childhood Education."[101] This plan reflected a basic belief of New Democrats that government should intervene in the marketplace to ensure equal opportunity in the pursuit of jobs. Of particular importance is intervening in the early of education of children from social groups with low high school graduation rates. The 2004 Democratic Platform recognized that, "Vast achievement gaps persist in America. Nearly half of African-American, Latino, and American Indian youth don't graduate high school."[102] The Platform suggested that one solution to this problem is improving early childhood education: "We believe in the potential of every child and we will not accept this loss of talent. Because education in the earliest years of a child's life is critical, we will expand and improve preschool and Head Start initiatives with the goal of offering these opportunities to all children."[103]

The Progressive Policy Institute's plan for expanding early childhood education is designed to prepare 4-year-old children to compete in a global work force and contribute to national economic development. Federal guidelines would require a "*science-based curricula* emphasizing a strong focus on developing children's language, pre-literacy and other academic skills [emphasis added]."[104] The goals of the program for 4-year-olds is steeped in the language of human capital, including improving the child's "earning potential." The plan claims: "Quality preschool improves children's life chances and benefits society by increasing both long-term education outcomes and earning potential while reducing delinquency and the costs of remedial education."[105]

The plan calls for a comprehensive system of early childhood learning for "all 4-year-old children in the nation." This would be accomplished through a substantial federal investment in early childhood education and tuition charges that would be based on family income. Essentially, the financial plan turns the program into an early education for children of the poor. Under the plan, the federal government would provide grants to "enable states to offer preschool to all poor children and help non-poor families afford preschool on a sliding payment scale."[106]

The pre-school education of 4-year-olds would be aligned with state standards for grades kindergarten through high school. In order to ensure alignment with state standards, preschool programs would be designed at the state level within the framework of federal guidelines. According to the plan: "While a national preschool initiative must set clear guidelines, states should set specific curricula and program delivery models."[107] And, as mentioned previously, federal guidelines would require a "science-based" curricula.

States would be required to monitor the program through accountability standards. The plan rejects accountability measurements that use "a national standardized assessment" for using trained individuals "who know the child" and who "would evaluate performance on school readiness tasks in a natural context and environment."[108] Supposedly, this accountability system would ensure that 4-year-olds would be prepared to earn high incomes in a globalized labor force and contribute to national economic growth.

CONCLUSION:
IS NO CHILD LEFT BEHIND A POLITICAL PIPE DREAM?

Have politicians launched American schools into a turbulent sea of standards, testing, and government report cards without proof that these actions will actually result in Americans being employed in the highest paid jobs in the global economy? It is frightening that No Child Left Behind, with its expanded federal and state bureaucracies and their links to an ever-expanding testing industry, became law without any proof that it will work. This is an expensive and massive experiment in educational change. What proof does the Progressive Policy Institute have that a comprehensive preschool program for 4-year-olds that is aligned with state K-12 standards and governed by state accountability standards will actually result in an improved economy and higher lifetime earnings?

It requires a longitudinal study to prove that No Child Left Behind will deliver on its promises. This kind of study would have to follow students from kindergarten into the labor market and analyze their lifetime incomes in comparison to other global workers.

Why would politicians support such a massive and expensive educational change without proof that it will work? In part, I believe the answer can be found in Bill Clinton's initial involvement in the standards and testing movement; politically, it looks good and sells well to the voter, and it doesn't require a large infusion of money into the school system.

Also, there are a number of facts that can be pieced together to show that education does contribute to improved lifetime income and economic growth. However—and this is important—none of these facts prove that *state standards and testing improve lifetime income and cause economic growth*.

Here are some facts that support the relationship between education, income, and economic growth:

- As reported by the U.S. Census Bureau, personal income is related to level of education, with high school graduates earning less than college graduates.[109]
- International studies do show a relationship between national level of educational attainment and national per capita income.[110]

However, these facts take on a slightly different meaning when educational inflation is considered. An educational credential is of high economic value when it is scarce. For instance, a high school diploma is of greater economic value in a labor market that has only a few high school graduates. As the number of high school graduates increases, the economic value of high school diplomas declines. What happens as the number of college graduates increases? In 1994, the Economic Policy Institute announced that, for the first time in history, the value of a college diploma was declining. In 1993, the median hourly wage for male college graduates declined to $17.62 from an inflation-adjusted high of $18.16 in 1989.

Also, as a result of deskilling, some occupations might require less rather than more education. Economist David Gordan contends that the spread of computerized machine tools in manufacturing has had no impact on machine shop skill levels. Regarding office occupations, Gordan wrote, "Skill demands appear to have declined substantially—for typists, office equipment, and telephone operators, among others." The increasing inequality in wages between poorly educated and highly educated workers, Gordon argues, is primarily a result of corporate union busting and downsizing. Concerning the assumption that low wages are a result of workers not having the right skills (or skills mismatch), economists Frank Levy and Richard Murnan maintained, "As a positive proposition, evidence of an accelerating skills mismatch is weak." In other words, there is no skill mismatch or lack of skills by American workers if jobs are being deskilled by computerization.

Commenting on Levy and Murnan, Gordon wondered, "Have we found a modern version of the story about the emperor with no clothes?"

Some might argue that concerns about deskilling are not meaningful in a global marketplace. In the New Democratic paradigm, all Americans ideally would receive enough education to become symbolic analysts. There might be a limit, according to this reasoning, on the number of symbolic analysts in the U.S. labor pool, but there might not be a limit in a global labor market. In this scenario, all American workers could earn top wages as symbolic analysts while the rest of world's workers struggle on low wages as routine production workers and in-person servers.

Of course, all of the above is speculative since no one can predict the result of the current trend of companies moving around the world searching for cheap labor and workers moving around the globe searching for high wages, while, at the same time, nations try to erect barriers to immigration and attempt to keep businesses in their own countries.

Therefore, economic arguments do not necessarily prove that expanded educational opportunities will result in Americans commanding the highest wages and best jobs in the global workforce.

What about purely educational, rather than economic, justifications for No Child Left Behind? The most important educational fact is that there are *no* longitudinal studies that describe the *type of educated person* that will result from a system of schooling governed by federal and state educational standards and tests. There might be improvement in test scores, but this only shows that the system is better preparing people to do well on tests and not the overall results in the type of person being educated.

Some Japanese people complain that their educational system, which is based on government tests, results in an educated person who is conforming and lacks creativity.[111] Will a school system governed by No Child Left Behind also result in a similar product? Economists talk about the importance of lifelong learning so that workers can keep abreast of technological changes. Will federal and state accountability systems increase or decrease the desire and ability of graduates to engage in lifelong learning? Technological advances depend on creativity. Will standards and tests inhibit or expand the creative potential of students?

All of the above questions should have been answered before Democrats and Republicans decided to impose a rigid system of standards and standardized tests on American schools. No Child Left Behind is a costly and a massive experiment without any clear indication of its ultimate results.

Chapter 4

What's Left of the Left?
Ralph Nader, the Green Party,
the Rainbow Coalition,
and the National Organization
for Women

With the triumph of the New Democrats, the so-called "left" of the Democratic Party either remained in the party as a marginalized group or sought other political affiliations, such as with Ralph Nader's organization; the Green Party; the Rainbow Coalition; and/or the National Organization for Women. All of these groups were highly critical of No Child Left Behind. However, the Green Party was the only group calling for repeal of the legislation. In the first edition of this book, I emphasized the disarray existing among the differing factions of the "left" in the United States. However, in the 2000 Presidential election the left rallied around Green Party candidate Ralph Nader. A longtime consumer advocate, Nader was the first U.S. Presidential candidate to focus on the problems associated with a consumerist ideology. Nader's educational concern was with the impact of consumerist ideology on children and teenagers and the resulting undermining of democratic activism. In the 2004 election, Nader launched his own presidential campaign, running as an independent with vice presidential candidate Peter Miguel Camejo. Camejo is a financier, political activist, and environmentalist. The Green Party nominated David Cobb for President and Pat LaMarche for Vice President.

Nader and many other members of the left now consider consumerism to be the triumphant ideology of the modern world and globalization.[1] It is consumerism, not capitalism, they argue, that won the Cold War of the 20th century. Consumerism defeated communist ideology in the Soviet Union

91

because, quite simply, the Soviet government's economic planning could not produce consumer goods as well as the West.

Consumerist ideology assumes that the goal of the economic system is constant growth and consumption of products. Constant economic growth and consumption are considered devastating to the environment and the quality of human life. Within this framework, the goal of technological development is the production of new goods.

The production of new goods requires the creation of new human needs. In the United States, the development of the advertising profession and its techniques created consumer desires for a steady stream of new products. The global spread of advertising methods created a global consumer culture. Economists, such as Simon Patten in the early 20th century, argued that agricultural and industrial development would continually produce product surpluses. The only way the agricultural and industrial machinery could be maintained, Patten argued, was the creation of new needs. Later, corporations, such as General Motors, introduced the idea of planned obsolescence through advertising new styles and models.

Consequently, advertising not only creates a need for new products but also convinces consumers to abandon products that they own for similar products with different styling. Within the framework of the ideology of consumerism, personal identity and social status are attached to brand names. People proudly wear clothes with identifying brand names or drive cars that identify their personality or social status.

Working and spending are the central values of consumerist ideology. Constant consumption requires longer hours of work: This is the tragic irony of consumerism. Technological advances do not free people from work but instead make new products that require more work to purchase. For instance, technology could be used to produce durable goods and reduce hours at work.

Commodified leisure, as exemplified by movies, television, theme parks, video games, recreational products, and packaged travel, provide both an escape from work and a reason to work harder. People work harder so that they can buy such items as boats, golf clubs, the newest hiking gear, and tickets for travel on a cruise ship. The desire for commodified leisure fills the fantasy world of the worker. In turn, the consumption of leisure provides escape from the often-numbing quality of office and factory work.

What distinguishes capitalism from consumerism? Capitalism assumes that people make rational choices in a free market, whereas consumerism assumes that individual choices in the market are a result of the manipulation of desires. In turn, political choices are the result of the manipulation of desires through the media. Politicians rely on advertising, media experts, and spin doctors to present their political agenda. Political image takes the place of political substance.

RALPH NADER, CONSUMERISM, AND EDUCATION

During the 2000 presidential campaign, Nader made consumerism the focal point of his educational policies. His acceptance speech at the Green Party Convention on June 25, 2000, asserted that there is a responsibility "to ensure that our children are well cared for. This is an enormous undertaking because our children are now exposed to the most intense marketing onslaught in history."[2] This marketing offensive, Nader argued, involves "precise corporate selling ... beamed directly to children separating them from their parents, an unheard of practice formerly, and teaching them how to nag their beleaguered parents as unpaid salesman for companies. There is a bombardment of their impressionable minds."[3]

Nader linked the lack of political activism among youth to the commercialization of their minds. He argued that commodified leisure occupies more and more of children's time. This results, Nader contended, in youth not responding to the growing economic inequalities in the United States and between nations. "To the youth of America," Nader warned in his acceptance speech, "beware of being trivialized by the commercial culture that tempts you daily. I hear you saying often that you're not turned on to politics .... If you do not turn on to politics, politics will turn on you."[4]

For Nader, commodified leisure was both reducing political activity and interfering with the ability of children to learn. Nader argued, "Obviously, you see how our children are not learning enough history, they're not learning how to write. Their attention span is being shrunken by all this entertainment on TV and videos that are beamed to them."[5] In his nomination speech he contended that, "This does not prepare the next generation to become literate, self-renewing, effective citizens for a deliberative democracy."[6]

The problem, as Nader defined it, was corporate targeting of children as present and future consumers. He quoted Mike Searles, former president of Kids-R-Us: "If you own this child at an early age, you can own this child for years to come. Companies are saying, 'Hey, I want to own the kid younger and younger.'"[7] To prove his point, he quoted a *Los Angeles Times* interview with Nancy Shalek, president of the Shalek Agency: "Advertising at its best is making people feel that without their product, you're a loser. Kids are very sensitive to that .... You open up emotional vulnerabilities and it's very easy to do with kids because they're the most emotionally vulnerable."[8]

The undermining of parental authority, according to Nader, was the goal of advertisers and their paid child psychologists. The process begins as early as age 2, with companies marketing directly to children. Boys and girls under the age of 12, Nader claimed, were responsible for spending $25 billion a year. Nader contended that marketers use three methods to "avoid or neutralize parental authority":

First, they urge the child to nag the parents.

Second, the sellers take conscious advantage of the absence of parents who are commuting and working long hours away from home.

Third, the marketers know that if they can undermine the authority, dignity, and judgment of parents in the eyes of their children, the little ones will purchase or demand items regardless of their parents' opinions.[9]

Also, Nader was disturbed by the effects of advertising and media on the present and future health of children. For instance, he argued that there was a direct link between teenage drinking and car crashes, suicide, date rapes, and problems teenagers have had in school and with their parents. Despite these problems, the alcohol industry advertises to audiences, according to the Federal Trade Commission, that include children, and the industry places their products in PG and PG-13 films that appeal to children and teenagers. In addition, the alcohol industry advertised on 8 of the 15 television shows that were most popular with adolescents. Advertising led to teenage smoking; for instance, the Marlboro Man, Nader claimed, appealed to teenage desires for independence.[10]

Violence, Nader contends, is presented to children and teenagers through movies, television, and video games. Nader quoted Lt. Col. Grossman, coauthor of *Stop Teaching Our Kids to Kill,* that shooter video games such as Duke Nukem, Time Crisis, and Quake "teach children the motor skills to kill, like military training devices do. And then they turn around and teach them to like it like the military would never do."[11]

Also, according to Nader, children's health has been undermined by a "barrage of ads for Whoppers, Happy Meals, Coke, Pepsi, Snickers bars, M&M's, and other junk foods and fast foods."[12] These marketing efforts contribute to the rise of child and teenage obesity and diabetes. Heath risks associated with severe obesity among children, Nader claimed, doubled since the 1960s. Now, he argued, 25%–30% of children are clinically obese.

Nader criticized schools for developing a consumer culture. He pointed to the widespread use of Chris Whittle's Channel 1 broadcasts in classrooms around the country. Whittle, it should be noted, is also the major stockholder in the for-profit school franchise The Edison Project. The program reaches, according to Nader, 8 million middle school, junior high, and high school students in 12,000 schools. The total time spent by students watching Channel 1 in 1 year was equivalent to about 1 class week. A 10-minute news broadcast on Channel 1 contained 2 minutes of commercials. Joel Babbit, former president of Channel 1, stated that "we are forcing kids to watch two minutes of commercials."[13]

Nader criticized Channel 1's role in promoting consumerism. Nader argued, "What Channel One really conveys is materialism: that buying is good and will solve your problems, and that consumption and self-gratification are the goals and ends of life."[14] Nader argued that many of Channel 1's commercials:

> ... promote low-grade sensuality to children as young as 11. Chew Winterfresh gum and kiss the Winterfresh babe. Shave with Schick razors and the Schick babe will hug you. There are ads for Blockbuster Video that portray kids playing video games nonstop for five days until they pass out from exhaustion. A Mountain Dew ad glorifies reckless driving. A Twix candy bar ad shows kids avoiding the consequences of doing badly at school by sending their report cards to the Eskimos so their parents won't read them. There are ads for Snickers that encourage kids to eat junk food. And then there are the ads, for products such as Gatorade, that show skinny models that make teenage girls feel badly about the way they look and encourage an unhealthy body image and an obsession with being thin.[15]

What is Nader's answer to the destruction of democracy through the commercialization of the minds of children and teenagers? First, he has argued that Congress should repeal Public Law 96-252, which prohibits the Federal Trade Commission from establishing rules to the protect children from commercial advertising. Second, he has appealed for a coalition of groups, including conservative organizations such as the Eagle Forum and Family Research Council, to work for laws to protect children from advertising and limit the access of marketing groups such as Channel 1 to public schools. Third, he has urged citizens to join the Center for a New American Dream, which is dedicated to overthrowing the ideology of consumerism. He recommended that citizens obtain the Center for a New American Dream's pamphlet, "Tips for Parenting in a Commercial Culture."

The Nader campaign also stressed the issue of child poverty, contending that 20% of children in the U.S. lived in poverty—a figure much higher than that for any other Western country. In addition, there is a direct link, Nader contended, between childhood poverty and school performance and, consequently, expectations for future earnings. Childhood poverty contributes, Nader argued, to the perpetuation of poverty. Nader called for more expanded health and welfare programs for children that would be paid for out of the future budget surplus of the federal government. Attacking Gore's Presidential candidacy, Nader argued that Gore proposed to "spend 88 percent of the projected budget surplus over the next decade on three accounts: Medicare, Social Security and private pension subsidies. Children are clearly not a priority. They are given only lip service and symbolic federal programs—and photo opportunities."

Nader was the first Presidential candidate to directly attack the ideology of consumerism and propose an educational agenda that included the protection of children and teenagers from indoctrination into consumerist values. This protection was to be combined with the teaching of an anti-consumerist ideology that included environmental education. In addition,

Nader urged government programs to eliminate childhood poverty. The combination of these efforts, Nader believed, would result in a generation dedicated to hands-on participation in democratic processes.

NADER'S 2004 CAMPAIGN

Accused of being a spoiler by those wanting to oust President Bush from the White House, Nader launched his own independent campaign in 2004. Leaders of the Democratic Party were not happy about Nader's independent candidacy because they feared it would help Bush's reelection campaign by siphoning votes away from John Kerry. Chairman of the Democratic National Committee, Terence R. McAuliffe pleaded with Nader, "As you consider whether to enter the race for President this year, I ask you to keep the best interest of the country—and the issues for which you have been an articulate, effective and passionate advocate—in mind. I ask you to stand united with the millions of Americans who yearn for change, who yearn to have their government and their country back."[16] Nader's response was that neither the Republican or Democratic Parties offered a real alternative to corporate control of America. He replied to McAuliffe:

> But while your kind letter received in early February properly took to task the Republican moneyed interests and their selected President George W. Bush, it did not respond to my agenda inquiry at all. Once again, I'm sorry to say, the exclusionary nature of the two-party duopoly diminishes basic dialogues on public policies affecting the common good …. The Party [Democratic] needs all the ideas and strategies, fully in the public domain, that can help improve this country. It needs to be pulled away from the corporate supremacists who have so seriously weakened the Party's appeal to working families everywhere.[17]

Nader illustrated his differences with the two major parties in a campaign brochure titled, "Let the Debate Begin!" The brochure asserted:

Declare Your Independence

George Bush and John Kerry are saying:

- No to a living wage
- No to health care for all
- No to major tax relief for working people
- No to real political reform
- No to ending the war, and
- No to the millions of Americans who hope for and need these changes.[18]

While Nader felt the Democratic Party was controlled by corporations, his major target was President George W. Bush. On April 13, 2004, Nader issued a press release calling for the impeachment of President Bush and Vice President Cheney. The press release demanded: "The Impeachment Inquiry should focus on two areas involving President Bush and Vice President Dick Cheney ... The unconstitutional war in Iraq ... [and] Five Falsehoods that Led to the Iraq Quagmire." The lengthy press release concluded, "Nader urges the Congress to investigate the illegal nature of the war, and how the five falsehoods became part of the Bush Administration's drum beat for war, in a formal Inquiry of Impeachment."[19]

NADER AND NO CHILD LEFT BEHIND

While sharply attacking the accountability requirements of No Child Left Behind, the 2004 Nader campaign continued to attack the effect of consumerism on children and commercialism in schools. Nader urged the federal government to promote a civic education program for Grades K-12 that would counter the influence of consumerism. A Nader campaign press release called for a new civic education for "an era when children are overwhelmed with marketing images that reduce their attention spans and vocabulary and orient them to an overweening focus on immediate gratification, low-grade sensuality and conspicuous consumption."[20]

One might assume that the goal of Nader's proposed civics program would be to educate citizens who would be, like Nader, actively working to improve society. Contrary to the student passivity that might result from an emphasis on testing and standards, the Nader campaign proposes, "And the government should encourage schools to infuse their curriculum with a citizenship emphasis that teaches students both how to *connect civic skills classroom learning to the outside world and how to practice democracy*."[21] The Nader campaign claims that "an emphasis on civics for democracy promises instead to take students from instruction to learning to knowledge to application until the highest educational goal is reached—the sustained onset of educational self-renewal of, by and for the confident, motivated student."[22]

However, the advocacy of an activist civics education program takes second place in Nader's campaign to criticisms of privatization and standardized testing. "The Nader campaign," a press release stated, "opposes the over reliance on high stakes standardized tests included in the federal Elementary and Secondary Education Act, commonly known as 'No Child Left Behind.'"[23] Nader criticizes the use of test scores to determine school funding and the retention and graduation of students. Nader's campaign material claims the following negative consequences from an overreliance on standardized testing:

- Use of single (limited) rather than multiple (comprehensive) measures of assessment.
- Excessive time devoted to narrow test preparation.
- Negative, unnecessary, and often lasting labeling of children.
- De-enrichment of the curriculum.
- False accountability.[24]

Unlike other political parties, the Nader campaign made direct reference to professional educational organizations. Many in these organizations have been critical of the effect of No Child Left Behind's accountability on classroom teaching. Teaching to the test, according to some, violates basic best practices in teaching. The Nader campaign asserted that standardized testing causes: "Movement away from widely accepted standards of teaching principles of best practice as articulated by the National Council of Teachers of Mathematics, National Council of Teachers of English, National Science Teachers Association, National Association for the Education of Young Children, and American Education Research Association."[25]

The Nader campaign claimed that No Child Left Behind was actually having a negative effect on the emotional development of children. "No Child Left Behind," Nader's campaign literature stated, "is counter-educational and a narrow gauge of assessment, and, for tens of thousands of children, highly deleterious to their emotional and intellectual development movement [sic] is unfair to poorer children from devastating backgrounds."[26]

An important complaint of the Nader campaign is that No Child Left Behind is channeling money away from basic educational needs to the coffers of the commercial testing industry. None of the other political parties leveled this charge against the legislation. In its list of complaints about testing, the Nader campaign charged: "Excessive use of financial resources for testing." Nader declared, "The federal government must not impose useless, costly and counterproductive mandates on schools—for example, it should discourage, not demand, the use of misleading and narrow multiple choice standardized tests."[27]

Rather than wasting money on standardized testing, testing that detracts from an activist civic education program, the Nader campaign argued that the money could be better spent on educational needs. "The United States stands now as the overall richest nation in the history of the world," claimed Nader's campaign literature. "There is no excuse for not smartly investing sufficient resources in education—an investment which, incidentally, pays off for society even in narrow monetary terms. Even the rest rooms for the children are often broken, filthy and devoid of privacy."[28] Under the banner, "Enough slogans and distractions!," Nader urged that federal funds be spent on the following priorities:

- Immediately provide full funding for Head Start.
- Guarantee pre-school education for all children.
- Adequately fund nutrition programs in the schools.
- Ensure that the nation's crumbling schools are repaired within three years.[29]

In summary, the 2004 Nader campaign retained its concerns with the effect of consumerism on children and the need for an activist civics education program, while focusing the majority of its educational discussion on the effects of standardized testing on school costs, classroom teaching, children's development, and children from low-income families. Unlike Democratic and Republican politicians, who could not politically afford to criticize the accountability sections of No Child Left Behind since they had supported this approach since the 1980s, Nader was able to give voice to those in the education community who did not believe that testing and standards would improve schools. In fact, many, like Nader, believed the accountability system was having a negative effect on classroom practices.

THE 2004 GREEN PARTY AND NO CHILD LEFT BEHIND

Not surprisingly given the confusing syntax of "No Child Left Behind," the 2004 Green Party Platform called the legislation "Leave No Child Behind" in its declaration: "The Leave No Child Behind Act must be repealed, especially the section that gives the military access to student records."[30] This makes the Green Party the only political party that clearly calls for repealing the legislation. Why? Because of the Green Party's position on democracy, noncompetitive education, and intellectual freedom in schools.

No Child Left Behind is particularly offensive to the Green party because of the party's dedication to local democracy. No Child Left Behind is a major intrusion in the affairs and control of local schools. Concern about political activism is a key element in the Green party agenda. The Green party's position on government reform is sometimes hard for citizens to understand, because the word *democracy* has frequently been used to describe the U.S. government system. The confusion is over the differences between representative government and direct democracy. The democratic aspect of representative government is the right of citizens to vote for their representatives. The Green party believes that elected representatives limit the ability of citizens to decide important issues. The 1996 Green platform explained it in these words:

> Greens advocate direct democracy as a response to local needs and issues, where all concerned citizens can discuss and decide questions that immediately affect their lives, such as land use, parks, schools and community ser-

vices. We hold as a "key value" GRASSROOTS DEMOCRACY and, as such, would decentralize many state functions to the country level and seek expanded roles for neighborhood boards/associations.[31]

The 2004 Green party platform stressed the importance of civil organizations. In its opening section of "Democracy," the Platform stated, "The power of civic action is an antidote to the corporate control of so much of our law-making …. We support citizen involvement at all levels of the decision-making process and hold that nonviolent direct action can be an effective tool."[32] The Platform supported a range of reforms to strengthen democracy, from campaign finance to abolishing the Electoral College. Of particular importance for education is its advocacy of Children's Parliaments: "We call for the implementation of Children's Parliaments, whereby representatives are elected by students to discuss, debate and make proposals to their city councils, school boards, county legislative bodies on a local level, to state legislatures statewide, and to Congress nationally."[33] Also, in the spirit of democracy, the platform proclaimed, "Young people should have input into the direction and pace of their own education, including input into the operation of their educational institutions."[34] The Green Party is the only political party to suggest that "youth" have a right to an education "that is stimulating, relevant, engaging, and that fosters their natural desire to learn."[35]

The emphasis on local democracy is reflected in their proposal to create schools governed by a council of teachers and parents with state and federal governments simply providing operating funds. Federal policy, the platform stated, "should act principally to ensure equal access to a quality education."[36] Regarding local control of schools, the Platform called for "equitable state and national funding for education and the creation of schools controlled by parent-teacher governing bodies."[37]

The Green party also rejects No Child Left Behind because of its potentially destructive effect on student creativity and the possibility that a reliance on test scores will encourage competitive education. The first proposal of the Platform's education section is: "We advocate creative and noncompetitive education at every age level, and the inclusion of cultural diversity in all curricula."[38] In addition, the Green party members feel that standards and testing restrict classroom methods. The party platform stated, "We encourage hands-on approaches that promote a multitude of individual learning styles."[39]

The Green party's commitment to local democracy includes a belief in the importance of intellectual and artistic freedom. The accountability and standards requirements of No Child Left Behind reduce intellectual freedom in schools by rigidly defining curriculum requirements. In contrast, the opening statement of the education section of the 2004 Green party platform clearly supports intellectual freedom in schools. This is a unique aspect of the party's approach to education. "Greens support educational diversity," the section opens. "We hold no dogma absolute, continually striving for truth in the realm of ideas."[40]

Consequently, as part of its general support of intellectual diversity, the Green party supports educational choice but only between different forms of public schools. It rejects privatization and vouchers that pay for students to attend private schools. The platform contends that vouchers for private schools will not only drain money away from public schools and create "a separate and unequal educational system."[41] "We also oppose charter schools," the platform states, "or the administration of public schools by private, for-profit entities."[42]

The Green party openly rejects the restrictions in No Child Left Behind on the distribution of birth control devices in schools and it rejects the federal government's stress on abstinence education:

> Targeting the young for age-appropriate education about AIDS/HIV and appropriate methods of prevention. We support sex education and the distribution of condoms in schools.[43]

> There must be access to free birth control devices, information counseling, and clinics to all who desire them. We call for implementation of family planning education for both genders in all levels of the state school system.[44]

While rejecting No Child Left Behind, the Green Party does accept the argument that education is key to economic development and that students should be prepared for lifelong learning. Consequently, the Green party calls for "tuition-free post secondary (collegiate and vocational) public education."[45] Regarding its stand for free post-secondary education, the platform stated, "In an economy that demands higher skills and a democracy that depends on an informed, educated electorate, opportunities for universal higher education and life-long learning must be vastly expanded."[46]

While Nader no longer leads the Green Party, concerns about consumerism and commercialism remained in the 2004 Platform: "We are deeply concerned about the intervention in our schools of corporations that promote a culture of consumption and waste. Schools should not be vehicles for commercial advertising."[47] In the introduction to its social justice section, the platform asserted, "We seek to protect our children from the corrosive effects of mass culture that trains them to regard themselves first and foremost as consumers."[48]

The Green party is the only American political party that devotes a large section of its platform to the arts. It links the arts to ideas of democratic empowerment, environmentalism, and cultural diversity. The platform's Arts platform is the second part of its education section, and it opens in the spirit of intellectual freedom: "Freedom of artistic expression is a fundamental right and a key element in empowering communities, and in moving us toward sustainability and respect for diversity."[49] Consequently, the platform uniquely proposed that arts education be incorporated into every aspect of the school curriculum, including math and science: "Funding and staffing to incorporate arts education into every school curriculum. We encourage local artists and the community to contribute time, experience, and resources to the effort."[50] The Platform spelled out instructional methods that should be used in arts education:

> Diversity in arts education in the schools including age-specific hands-on activities and appreciative theoretical approaches, exposure to the arts of various cultures and stylistic traditions, and experiences with a variety of media, techniques and contents. The integration of the arts and artistic teaching methods into other areas of the curriculum to promote a holistic perspective.[51]

Of course, the Green party places a strong emphasis on environmental education. In its social justice section, the Platform stated, "We advocate a diverse system of education that would introduce children early to the wonders of the *Great School* (Nature), and would cultivate the wisdom of eco-education, eco-economics, eco-politics, and eco-culture."[52]

THE RAINBOW COALITION

"Democrats for the Leisure Class"—that is what Jesse Jackson calls the New Democrats and Democratic Leadership Council.[53] As founder and national field director of the Rainbow Coalition, Jackson is an outspoken critic of efforts by the Democratic Leadership Council and the New Democrats to push the Democratic party to the center of the political spectrum. Running for the Democratic Presidential nomination in 1984, he tried to keep the party focused on liberal concerns about the rights of labor, inequalities in wealth, and racial and gender equity.[54] From Jackson's perspective, "the Democratic Leadership Conference [sic]—'the moderate' Democratic organization [that was] formed to offset the influence of the National Rainbow Coalition after the 1984 presidential campaign ... [wanted] to appeal to white males and pull the Democratic Party back to the center."[55]

Losing the struggle over the direction of the Democratic party to the New Democrats, Jackson remained the best-known progressive voice in the Democratic party. Jackson warned that "the only counter to prevent Clinton from caving in to the Republican right and conservatives in his own party, if he is to be countered, is his base—people of color, workers, women and progressives."[56]

As the progressive voice of the Democratic party Jackson is outspoken in his criticism of the Christian Coalition. He charges the Christian Coalition with being an exclusionary organization and observed that "their mean-spiritedness is not limited to Blacks. There are no Jews in the 'Christian Coalition,' by definition."[57] Warning of the dangers of the right, Jackson asserted, "If this were Germany, we would call it fascism. If this were South Africa, we would call it apartheid. In America we call it conservatism. And it provides a cover for a public policy of scapegoating, exclusion, and distrust."[58]

Regarding education, Jackson and the Rainbow Coalition support a continuation of the 1960s' liberal education agenda, including war-on-poverty programs, Affirmative Action, remedial education, Head Start, day care, and parental involvement in schools. This liberal model assumes that equality of educational opportunity is the key to providing economic opportunity. On the surface, the Rainbow Coalition's educational policies are similar to those of the New Democrats. Below the surface are profound differences.

Affirmative Action is one important difference. Hoping to win back White men to the Democratic party, New Democrats support a race- and gender-neutral policy for Affirmative Action. In contrast, the Rainbow Coalition and their ally, the National Organization for Women (NOW), reject a race- and gender-neutral policy. The leaders of these two organizations want Affirmative Action to correct racial and gender imbalances by considering existing balances. For instance, if a college does not have any African American faculty members, then the college should actively recruit African Americans. A race- and gender-neutral policy would not try to correct existing racial and gender imbalances; instead it would try to avoid racial and gender discrimination. Throughout this chapter I use the term *positive Affirmative Action* to indicate policies that consciously attempt to correct existing imbalances.

Affirmative Action as a legal policy originated with the passage of the 1964 Civil Rights Act, which prohibited discrimination based on race, color, religion, sex, or national origin. In 1965, President Lyndon Johnson issued an executive order requiring federal agencies to "maintain a positive program of equal opportunities."[59] A "positive program" was interpreted to mean that the race and gender of a job applicant should be considered during the hiring process in order to achieve a fair racial and gender balance in employment.

According to the Rainbow Coalition and NOW, equal educational opportunity is rendered meaningless unless there are positive Affirmative-Action hiring practices. Equal educational opportunity is also meaningless unless there are positive Affirmative-Action college admission policies. If there are no positive Affirmative-Action programs for hiring faculty members, then female and racial minority students are denied positive role models in elementary and secondary schools and colleges.

Both the Rainbow Coalition and NOW contend that there is legal precedent for positive Affirmative-Action policies in education. In the famous Bakke decision, the U.S. Supreme Court, while ruling against the Affirmative-Action admissions policy of the medical school of the University of California, found that "race conscious" admissions policies were constitutional. In 1989, the U.S. Supreme Court ruled as constitutional the Affirmative-Action hiring program of the Aluminum and Chemical Corporation that set aside half its trainee positions for African Americans until racial parity was reached. Other Affirmative-Action quota programs have also been ruled constitutional.[60]

Therefore, unlike the New Democrats, the Rainbow Coalition considers positive Affirmative-Action programs essential for ensuring equality of educational opportunity and equality of opportunity in the workplace as well as for providing racial minorities and women with positive role models in educational institutions.

Unlike many on the right, the Rainbow Coalition retains a belief in the possibility of equal educational opportunity overcoming educational problems caused by poverty. The debate sparked by Richard Herrnstein and Charles Murray's book *The Bell Curve* underscores the differing attitudes regarding education and poverty. Under the colorful title "Let Them Eat Grits: Pseudo-Intellect Mixes Race, IQ to Justify America's Ethnic Cleansing," Jackson asserted that "Charles Murray has cleverly packaged and promoted a new book that will be an unread bestseller .... The conservative polemicist will pocket a small fortune huckstering a pseudointellectual justification for the affluent to feel no responsibility for the wretched." Using what Jackson calls pseudoscientific methods, Herrnstein and Murray not only relieved the rich of any guilt about the poor but justified beliefs that "attempts to alleviate their misery are doomed to failure. Affirmative action should be repealed, remedial education abandoned."[61]

In his review of *The Bell Curve* Jackson argued that paying for the Vietnam war reduced funding for the war on poverty and destroyed any possibility of its success. The continued cost of the cold war, or what Jackson called "the most expensive peace time military buildup in the annals of time," further exacerbated the problem of poverty. "Those in barrios and ghettos," Jackson complained, "were left more segregated and wretched than ever. Today 45% of all Black children live at or below poverty in destructive conditions lacking prenatal care, nutrition, immunization, safe homes, decent neighborhoods."[62]

To save children living in poverty, Jackson argues, requires full funding of war-on-poverty programs or, as Jackson stated, "Why not earn and learn our way out of poverty?" In 1993, Jackson initiated the Rainbow National Reclaim Our Youth Crusade to build self-esteem and give direction to young people. In 1994, the organization created a Back-to-School Pledge asking a promise from parents to accompany their children on the first day of school, meet the child's teachers, pick up report cards, and turn off the television for 3 hours a night. Another organizational project, the Youth Empowerment Committee, creates opportunities for youth to investigate and debate issues involving urban poverty, while the Courts and Justice Committee attempts to keep youth out of jail.[63]

Fulfilling of the liberal agenda of the war on poverty, Jackson believes, is possible. Adequate prenatal care for women, good nutrition, and medical care for infants combined with quality Head Start and daycare programs will, Jackson argues, give children born into poverty an equal opportunity to learn when they enter school. Remedial education programs will help children overcome learning problems. The Back-To-School Pledge will foster parental involvement in education and ensure that the home supports the work of the school. To complete the Rainbow Coalition's educational agenda, positive Affirmative-Action policies will ensure that faculties can provide positive role models for all students, that school graduates are given an equal opportunity to enter college, and that equal educational opportunities result in an equal opportunity to get a job.

By the 2004 election, Jesse Jackson's concerns were more on criticizing George W. Bush and economic issues than on education. On February 17, 2004, he defined the future of the Rainbow Coalition in a speech, "How to Keep Hope Alive: the Future of the Rainbow Coalition" to the John F. Kennedy Jr. Forum at the Harvard University Institute of Politics. Jackson opened the speech by defending the actions of the Rainbow Coalition as a "counter-cultural" movement. He argued that counter-cultural movements in the United States are important in the fight for those excluded from society to gain inclusion, such as helping to "Abolish slavery, End legal segregation, Seek gender equality, Women's right to vote, Worker's right to organize, Freedom to debate and participate in foreign policy."[64] Formed during the 1984 presidential election, the Rainbow Coalition, Jackson claimed, brought together "African Americans, Latinos, Asian and other people of color, with the peace and nuclear freeze movements, and others engaged in fighting 'Reaganism' of the 1980s."[65] The historic goal of the Rainbow Coalition, Jackson asserted, was creating a level playing field so that all people could have equality of opportunity.

However, a level playing field requires protection of the economic interests of the people. "Wal-Mart," Jackson argued, "is a Confederate Trojan Horse. On the outside of the horse, the name means cheap prices. Inside the horse, it means cheap wages, no health benefits, crushing small vendors and losing jobs to slave-wages overseas."[66] The Bush administration's domestic and foreign policies, Jackson claimed, resulted in "passing on unfunded mandates to the states [No Child Left Behind being one of those mandates], downsizing the middle class, expanding poverty and creating a record North/South divide between surplus culture and deficit culture."[67]

Against the background of what Jackson considered the tragedy of Bush administration policies, Jackson called for a new era of hope: "We must build a multicultural rainbow coalition. We must revive hope. We must revive hope in the vote, and urge massive voter registration."[68] The next stage of the struggle, Jackson argued, was gaining access to capital: "As workers, investors, consumers and taxpayers, we have the capacity to demand that at least 5% of these assets [corporate] be managed by people of color."[69] In other words, education can help level the playing field, but it requires money in the United States to ensure that the field is truly level.

The acquisition of capital, Jackson considered as the next stage in the struggle for equality. "We need to expand our vision beyond politics," Jackson told his 2004 Harvard audience, "and recognize that the battle is now on the economic front. Our struggle can be defined in four stages":

1. Ending slavery.
2. Ending segregation.
3. Achieving the right to vote.
4. Access to capital.[70]

THE NATIONAL ORGANIZATION FOR WOMEN AND THE FEMINIST MAJORITY

Similar to the Rainbow Coalition, the National Organization for Women was furious at the actions of the Bush administration. The organization's 2004 Web site contains a special section called "The Truth About George." "Piece by piece," it is proclaimed in The Truth About George, "Bush is tearing down the progress women and other disenfranchised groups have made over the last 35 years, ensuring that rich white males and giant corporations will rule the U.S. for generations to come."[71] Regarding education, the organization expressed concern about the underfunding of No Child Left Behind and a 2002 proposal by the U.S. Department of Education's Office of Civil Rights to support single-sex schools and classes.

In 1966, the National Organization for Women issued its founding words: "There is no civil rights movement to speak for women as there has been for Negroes and other victims of discrimination. The National Organization for Women must therefore begin to speak."[72] With these historic words in 1966, NOW joined the civil rights movement and assumed political leadership that would transform public schools. Like the Rainbow Coalition, NOW is critical of the New Democratic movement. Describing its membership as "feminists and progressives" at a 1996 demonstration in front of the White House, NOW president Patricia Ireland ridiculed President Bill Clinton for the passage and signing of new welfare legislation. "The so-called 'pro-family' Congress," Ireland proclaimed, "churned out a law that will destroy poor families. And now the so-called 'new Democrat' in the White House signed it."[73] After attacking the Republican Congress and the New Democrats, Ireland turned her attention to the power of the religious right with these words: "Bill Clinton is only the most recent politician to stagger to the right after an onslaught of immoral attacks by the highly organized religious and political extremists, ... and we see the radical right's ability to raise money and defeat progressive candidates—often with the aid and assistance of churches."[74]

At a "Fight the Right" San Francisco rally in 1996, Ireland acknowledged unity with other progressive organizations, including the Rainbow Coalition, in opposing the religious right, neoconservatives, and the New Democrats. Of particular concern to NOW was the attempt to end positive Affirmative-Action policies. "In California, the Congress and everywhere in between," Ireland declared, "we're going to squash the right wing's jaded attempt to roll back decades of progress on affirmative action and other issues. The vehemence of their attacks is an ironic indicator of our success over the years."[75]

Ireland's reference to "our success" is an accurate evaluation of NOW's accomplishments in schools and colleges. Over the years, NOW has been a strong political force for the following goals:

1. Ensuring equal access for women to educational programs such as science, mathematics, vocational, and athletics.
2. Creating nonsexist learning materials.
3. Creating learning materials that increase females' self-esteem.
4. Breaking down the exclusionary walls of all-male schools.
5. Establishing women's studies programs.
6. Reducing the sexist bias in high-stakes tests.
7. Creating affirmative-action college admission programs for women.
8. Creating affirmative-action faculty-hiring programs.
9. Protecting female faculty members from discriminatory practices in the college tenure process.

The 1966 Statement of Purpose, coauthored by Betty Friedan, author of *The Feminine Mystique*, and Dr. Pauli Murray, an African American Episcopal minister, placed NOW's educational efforts in a general struggle to achieve "a fully equal partnership of the sexes ... [and a] full participation [of women] in the mainstream of American society ... exercising all the privileges and responsibilities thereof in truly equal partnership with men."[76] Friedan and Murray contended that women with an average life span of nearly 75 years no longer devote the greatest part of their lives to childrearing. Furthermore, they asserted, muscular strength, because of technological advances, is no longer "a criterion for filling most jobs."[77] Therefore, they argued, "In view of this new industrial revolution created by automation in the mid-twentieth century, women must participate in old and new fields of society in full equality—or become permanent outsiders."[78] The Statement of Purpose provided evidence of sex segregation in the labor market, discriminatory wage differences between men and women, and the small numbers of women as compared to men graduating from college and professional schools. In response to these data, Friedan and Murray called for the effective enforcement of American law and the Constitution to end patterns of sex discrimination, to provide equality of civil and political rights, and "to ensure equality of opportunity in employment and education."[79]

Calling education "the key to effective participation in today's economy," the writers of NOW's original Statement of Purpose demanded that public schools educate every young woman "to her full potential of human ability."[80] Of primary concern to the writers was raising female expectations for achievement in school and for pursuing professional degrees. The document identified the following educational problems confronting women:

1. Discriminatory quotas in college and professional school admissions.
2. Lack of encouragement by parents, counselors, and teachers.
3. Denial of fellowships and loans to women.
4. Traditional procedures in professional training geared to men.
5. Lack of attention to female school dropouts.

NOW's Task Force on Education issued its report in 1967. The report's primary concern was to raise the aspiration levels of females at every level of schooling and limit the influence of traditional sex-oriented self-concepts. Besides changing the sex-role stereotypes found in schools, the task force commended the activities of the NOW Task Force on Media. The NOW Task Force on Education proposed placing articles in professional journals, pressuring school administrators, and contacting parents and the Parent-Teacher Association.[81]

The turning point in NOW's education efforts came in 1972 with the passage of Title IX of the Higher Education Act. The legislation provided for sexual equality in all educational institutions, including preschool classrooms, elementary and secondary schools, vocational and professional schools, and public and private undergraduate and graduate schools. Armed with the legal power of Title IX, NOW began a national campaign for its enforcement. Local NOW chapters sued local school systems. The first important lawsuit by a local chapter of NOW was against the 13 school systems in Essex County, New Jersey. The local NOW chapter accused the school systems of maintaining sex-segregated courses in home economics and industrial arts.[82]

In 1974, NOW defeated efforts by the National Collegiate Athletic Association to omit sports from the coverage of Title IX. Consequently, 1975 federal regulations were created to bar sex discrimination in intercollegiate athletics. By 1976, NOW chapters across the country were using Title IX in lawsuits ranging from female participation in athletics to gender-biased hiring in school administration. Also, in 1975, NOW'S Legal and Defense Fund charged 40 states with violating federal requirements under Title IX.

By 1974, with help from NOW's Committee to Promote Women's Studies, more than 1,000 colleges were offering women's studies courses and degree programs. Also, NOW began pressuring Congress for legislation allowing admission of women to military service academies. Under political pressure from NOW and other women's organizations, Congress passed the 1976 Educational Equity Act, which authorized the Office of Education to begin preparing "non-sexist curricula and non-discriminatory vocational and career counseling, sports education, and other programs designed to achieve equity for all students regardless of sex."[83]

In 1983, NOW proudly announced that "The last all-male school in the Ivy League became co-educational when Columbia College enrolled women for the first time in its 229-year history."[84] Sex bias in high-stakes testing became an issue in 1986 when NOW president Eleanor Smeal and other civil rights groups organized FairTest, a group that claimed that standardized tests referred twice as often to males and male activities compared to females and female activities. In 1987, FairTest claimed that the sex bias of the SAT and PSAT were denying female students fellowships and scholarships. During this period, NOW investigated charges of sex bias in college hiring and tenure practices.[85]

NOW's long-term hope is, in the words of NOW National Secretary Karen Johnson, "to finally raise sex discrimination to the same level of constitutional scrutiny as race."[86] NOW leaders pinned their hopes on a Supreme Court case challenging the male-only admission policy at the Virginia Military Institute. Although the Supreme Court's final decision left undecided the constitutional issue of race and sex discrimination being equivalent, the judgment did, according to Johnson, affirm that "the qualities important for military leaders—integrity, tenacity and bravery—have nothing to do with a person's sex."[87]

The Virginia Military Institute decision exemplifies the ways in which NOW and other feminist organizations have reshaped educational institutions. In 1996, the report "Opening Doors in Education" detailed the results of Title IX and Affirmative Action:

1. Female medical school graduates rose from 8.4% of the total medical school graduates in 1969 to 34.5% in 1990.
2. Women increased their share of doctoral and professional degrees from 14.4% of doctorates in 1971 to 36.8% in 1991.
3. Affirmative action and federal legislation increased women's opportunities in vocational education.
4. Female involvement in high school and college athletics increased with participation in high school athletics increasing from 7% in 1972 of the total number of students in athletics to 37% in 1992 and in college from 15.6% in 1972 to 34.8% in 1993.[88]

While citing these accomplishments, feminist leaders continued to worry about entrenched sex discrimination in higher education and vocational training, the disproportionate number of women without tenure or full professorships in higher education, and remaining barriers in athletics. The report defended the continued use of Affirmative Action in college admissions by suggesting that the real preferential treatment in college admissions goes to the "children of alumni—not women and minorities."[89] As proof, the report disclosed that "children of alumni at Harvard University in 1991 were three times more likely to be accepted than other prospective students. At Yale, children of alumni are two and a half times more likely to be admitted."[90] As part of the strategy to combat the right, Eleanor Smeal, the former president of NOW, organized the Feminist Majority in 1987 to help elect feminist candidates to Congress and state and local governments. Warning about the "unprecedented attack by right-wing extremists," the Feminist Majority issued a statement that "by proclaiming ourselves feminists, we emphasize what it means to stand up for women's rights, equality, and empowerment."[91] For the Feminist Majority, the significant issues remain equality for women, reproductive freedom, and increased human services.

By the 21st century, NOW and the Feminist Majority considered themselves in a powerful struggle against the religious right and Republicans. The most heated issue was abortion. Although abortion accounted for a major part of the political divide between feminist organizations and the right, education and Affirmative Action remained contentious items.

Calling it the revolt of "angry White males," the religious right, neoconservatives, and New Democrats oppose positive Affirmative-Action policies. Progressives within the Democratic Party claim that Affirmative-Action policies that do not take into consideration gender and racial balance will perpetuate discrimination. NOW and the Feminist Majority insist that race and gender considerations are a necessary part of Affirmative Action because conditions of bias against women continue to exist.

After years of struggle to ensure gender equity in public schools, leaders of the National Organization for Women were alarmed in 2002 when the Office of Civil Rights of the U.S. Department of Education issued a notice of its intention "to propose amendments to the regulations implementing Title IX ... to provide more flexibility for educators to establish single-sex classes and schools at the elementary and secondary schools ... and to provide public school parents with a diverse array of educational options."[92]

The organization accused Bush's Department of Education of basing this policy on an unproven assumption that equal opportunity for women can be protected when students are separated by gender. In a section of their response titled "Perpetuates Sex-Stereotyping and Feelings of Superiority/Inferiority," it is claimed: "Studies show that all-boys schools promote sexism and feelings of superiority toward women. Girls, as the traditionally subordinated group, are likely to experience a badge of inferiority as a result of being grouped on the basis of sex."[93] Also, the organization claimed that same-sex schooling would decrease workplace equity: "Depriving boys and girls of the opportunity to interact daily as peers in the classroom during their formative years will adversely affect gender relations in the adult workplace and in their lives."[94]

Unfortunately for the National Organization of Women and others struggling for gender equity in education, the U.S. Secretary of Education announced his intention on March 9, 2004 to allow single-sex classes and schools in the public school system. The announcement stated:

> The Secretary proposes to amend the regulations implementing Title IX of the Education Amendments of 1972 (Title IX), which prohibit sex discrimination in federally assisted education programs. These proposed amendments would clarify and modify Title IX regulatory requirements pertaining to the provision of single-sex schools and classes in elementary and secondary schools. The proposed amendments would expand flexibility for recipients that may be interested in providing single-sex schools or classes, and they would explain how single-sex schools or classes may be provided consistent with the requirements of Title IX.[95]

In reference to No Child Left Behind, the U.S. Secretary of Education stated that single-sex schools should be available as a parental choice: "the Secretary intends to propose amendments to our Title IX regulations in order to provide more flexibility to educators to establish single-sex schools and classes at the elementary and secondary levels and to provide additional public educational choices to parents."[96]

Instead of supporting single-sex classes and schools, the National Organization for Women demanded that the Bush administration attend to the following issues. In essence, these issues represent the educational concerns of the organization in 21st Century.

- Adequate funding to existing coeducational schools.
- Smaller class sizes.
- More diverse curriculum offerings to which all students have access.
- Gender equity training for administrators, teachers, counselors, and other staff.
- Sexual harassment training and improving support services for students who encounter sexual harassment.[97]

CONCLUSION: WHAT'S LEFT OF THE LEFT?

Do Nader's organization, the Green Party, the Rainbow Coalition, and the National Organization for Women represent what's left of the left in the United States after the New Democrats took over control of the Democratic Party? Picking over the bones of the liberal wing of the Democratic party after its demise at the hands of the New Democrats, Michael Tomasky, author and political commentator for *The Village Voice* and *New York* magazine, searched for policies that would restore to the left a cohesive political agenda. In *Left for Dead*, he contended that the liberal left's political efforts are hampered because by "speaking to people as members of groups—and only as members of groups—we've lost the ability to talk to the whole."[98] Using "left," "liberal left," and "progressive" interchangeably, Tomasky described the political dilemmas facing a wheelchair-bound African American lesbian. Which of her four identities—disabled, African American, woman, and lesbian—defines her politics? She has, Tomasky pointed out, other identities as a worker, commuter, purchaser of goods, renter or home-owner, and neighbor. "The left," Tomasky complained, "has been dogged about addressing her identity as female, Black, lesbian, and disabled, far less so about addressing the others."[99]

Tomasky's quest for a means of reunifying the left is in response to the abandonment of the Democratic party by voters who were alienated by the attention given to the poor and disenfranchised groups. What political policies can unite disparate groups, such as the wheelchair-bound African American lesbian, the African American male auto worker, the White female small farmer, and the Latina female office worker? Although he is aware of the special issues for minority cultures, women, gays and lesbians, and the disabled, Tomasky hopes that broader issues can be found to unite the progressive wing of the Democratic party.

What does Tomasky offer as the salvation of the liberal left? "The first principle," he proposed, "is to fight the new war: to produce a strategy to protect working families in the age of globalization."[100] Like the New

Democrats, Tomasky recognizes that the development of a global workforce is depressing U.S. wages. Yet, unlike the New Democrats, Tomasky does not want the global labor market to victimize workers. Tomasky is sickened by corporate leaders earning 45 times more than the wage of average workers. He suggests protecting workers by reducing the work week to 30 hours, giving workers control of their companies, reducing federal programs that provide welfare to corporations, increasing corporate taxes, reducing taxes on annual incomes below $80,000, and increasing taxes on incomes above $80,000. Higher corporate taxes— which declined over the last 40 years, from 38% to 13%—and taxes on high incomes, Tomasky maintains, would pay for reduced taxes on low incomes and government programs that would give U.S. workers adequate medical care, better public schools, and secure retirement programs. Topping the list of Tomasky's proposals for government reform is breaking the influence of money over political campaigns and legislative decisions. Regarding personal freedom, Tomasky supports gay and lesbian rights, freedom of speech, and the legal access to abortion.[101]

Tomasky offers a small agenda for uniting the left around school issues. Multiculturalism—despised by the right and ignored by New Democrats—continues as an important subject for progressives. Tomasky wants textbooks to include more history and information on minority cultures. "But this history," he insisted, "should be taught not out of pietistic concern for the self-esteem of minority children, as the left has posited, but simply because it is information that all American children, all future citizens should have."[102] Tomasky wants the left to assume leadership in raising academic standards and lengthening the school day and school year.

Today, the rallying point of the Left appears to be opposition to compassionate conservatives and neoconservatives. Regarding education, despite Tomasky's hope that it could be a unifying factor, the Left seems united in objections to No Child Left Behind, standards, and standardized testing. The only party on the Left with a clear vision for the future of public schools is the Green Party. Is the Green Party now the major party of the left?

Chapter 5

Putting It Together

No Child Left Behind includes policies pursued for many years by compassionate conservatives, neoconservatives, and New Democrats. I fear that national and state academic standards and tests will place a stranglehold on free thought. The immense political influence of the Christian Coalition and conservative think tanks will ensure that the content of these academic standards and tests will hew to a particular ideological line. At the 1996 History of Education meeting in Toronto, I asked neoconservative Diane Ravitch about the history standards. Stressing the importance of regulating the school curriculum, she answered, "I want the right attitudes developed by history instruction." What are the right attitudes? Who should have the power to determine these attitudes? As Austrian economists argue, the problem is not the existence of a particular ideology but the use of government to enforce that ideology.

The campaign for standards and standardized testing created a new class of educational experts to design and implement these instruments of control. These educational experts illustrate the symbiotic relationship between intellectuals and government. The test makers and standard writers depend on government support and therefore continue to supply ideological justification for government regulation of the content of schooling.

I admire the efforts of the religious right to create private schools that reflect their religious values, but I am disturbed and angered by their efforts to impose their values on the rest of the population. The problem is that the religious right believe they have a moral imperative to aggressively pursue evangelical policies that force all people to act as good Christians. Swept up by religious zeal, they could, along with advocates of standards and tests, make U.S. public schools the instruments of intellectual totalitarianism.

Choice, charter, and for-profit schools are meaningless if there is no intellectual diversity in the curriculum. Only the Green Party calls for intellectual diversity. These reform plans become a new means of achieving the

114

same goal of controlling what students learn. For-profit schools may be the new frontier of a consumer society. Brand names may replace traditional high school symbols on varsity sweaters.

I reject the idea that the primary purpose of schooling and education should be increasing economic competitiveness and improving workers' skills. I firmly believe that the goal of government and education should be maximization of human happiness. Thinking is pleasure. Schools have removed pleasure from thinking as they turn the human mind into a commodity to be used by global corporations.

What about the politics of culture? I believe the goal of multicultural education should be to explore other cultures for the purpose of evaluating and changing the values of our society. I do not believe that the only purpose is to create cultural tolerance. Coming from a long line of White Indians—Europeans who joined Indian tribes—I believe U.S. society can learn a great deal from Native American values about sharing wealth, about a human's place in nature, and about pleasure.

Only the Green party spoke out against the commercialization of American schools. Only the Green party focused on consumer issues as related to children and the consequences of a consumer culture for political activism. Only the Green party raised the issue of environmentalism in the context of consumerist ideology and suggested that children must be protected from the ideology that supports any environmentally destructive economic system. One would think that environmental education would be at the top of most political parties' educational agendas. However, environmental education might threaten corporations and reduce their financing of political campaigns. Unfortunately, environmentalism is political.

Table 5.1 compares and summarizes the conflicting and overlapping political positions on education. Obviously, the table cannot portray the complexity of the issues or the origins and strategies of organizations and groups such as compassionate conservatives, neoconservative, New Democrats, the Green Party, the Rainbow Coalition, and the National Organization for Women. Understanding the table requires a reading of the preceding chapters. Table 5.1 is intended to be a summary guide.

TABLE 5.1

Political Agendas for Education

Political Group	Attitudes Towards No Child Left Behind	Major Educational Concerns
Republican: Compassionate Conservative	Hesitant about massive federal involvement in local schools; primarily support sections dealing with character education, school prayer, Boy Scouts, abstinence education, ban on school birth control clinics, use of faith–based organizations, and choice plans.	Protection of religious values in schools, school choice, abstinence education.
Republican: Neoconservative	Support the legislation, particularly sections dealing with accountability, school choice, and for-profit companies.	Free market for schools with open competition between public schools and for-profit schools; education should be regulated by government standards and testing.
New Democrats	Favor accountability and public charter school sections of legislation.	Support reinventing the schools with choice provided by public charter schools; Support standards and testing; Oppose privatization, and faith-based initiatives.
Nader 2004	Attacks reliance on standardized testing; claims legislation channels educational monies away from needed school improvements to the testing industry.	Civic education courses that create activist citizens; consumerism and commercialism in education.
Green Party	Calls for repeal of legislation.	Intellectual and cultural diversity in schools; schools controlled by teachers and parents; public school choice; environmental education; arts education.
Rainbow Coalition	Rejects New Democrat's emphasis on educational accountability as means of school improvement.	Supports liberal education agenda, including war-on-poverty programs, Affirmative Action, remedial education, Head Start, day care, and parental involvement in schools.
National Organization for Women	Objects to inclusion of single-sex schools as part of choice options in legislation.	Gender equity.

Notes

CHAPTER 1

1. George W. Bush, *On God and Country*, edited by Thomas Freiling (Washington, DC: Allegiance Press, Inc., 2004), pp. 169–171.
2. Ibid., p. 122.
3. *No Child Left Behind Act of 2001, Public Law 107-110* (January 8, 2002) http://www.ed.gov/policy/elsec/leg/esea02/107-110.pdf.
4. George W. Bush, Comment on the front cover of Myron Magnet, *The Dream and the Nightmare: The Sixties' Legacy to the Underclass* (San Francisco: Encounter Books, 2000).
5. Magnet, *The Dream*, 20.
6. Ibid., p. 24.
7. Patrick J. Buchanan, *Right From the Beginning* (Washington, DC: Regnery Gateway, 1990), p. 14.
8. "Educational Policy Statement of Bush Campaign," retrieved from *http://www.georgebush.com*, 24 August 2000.
9. Marvin Olasky, *Renewing American Compassion* (Washington, DC: Regnery, 1997), pp. 41–42.
10. Ibid., p. 36
11. Ibid., pp. 29–30.
12. Patrick J. Buchanan, *Right From the Beginning* (Washington, DC: Regnery Gateway, 1990), p. 14.
13. William J. Bennett, *The De-Valuing of America: The Fight for Our Culture and Our Children* (New York: Simon & Schuster, 1992), p. 36.
14. Joel Spring, *The American School*, 6th ed. (New York: McGraw-Hill, 2005), pp. 44–102.
15. Bennett, *The De-Valuing of America*, p. 206.
16. Ralph Reed, *Active Faith: How Christians Are Changing the Soul of American Politics* (New York: The Free Press, 1996), p. 9.
17. Michael Lind, *Up From Conservatism: Why the Right Is Wrong for America* (New York: The Free Press, 1996), p. 154.
18. Ibid., p. 161.

19. Press Release, "Character Education Grants Awarded," (Washington, DC: U.S. Department of Education, September 29, 2003), http://www.ed.gov/news/pressreleases/2003/09/09292003.html.
20. Ibid.
21. Roderick Paige, "White House Conference on Faith-Based and Community Initiatives," http://www.ed.gov/news/speeches/2002/10/10102002.html.
22. Press Release, "Paige Names John Porter as Director of Department's Center for Faith-Based and Community Initiatives," (Washington, DC: U.S. Department of Education, May 29, 2002, 2003), http://www.ed.gov/news/pressreleases/2002/05/05292002a.html.
23. U.S. Department of Education, "No Child Left Behind and Faith-Based Leaders: Working Together So All Children Succeed" (Washington, DC: U.S. Government Printing Office, 2004), http://www.ed.gov/nclb/freedom/faith/leaders.pdf.
24. Ibid.
25. This message is given on the Christian Coalition's Web site, http://cc.org/about.html.
26. See Jacob Weisberg, *In Defense of Government: The Fall and Rise of Public Trust* (New York: Scribner's, 1996), and Michael Tomasky, *Left for Dead: The Life, Death and Possible Resurrection of Progressive Politics in America* (New York: The Free Press, 1996).
27. See Joel Spring, *The American School* ..., pp. 448–463.
28. Reed, *Active Faith*, p. 105.
29. Jacob Weisberg, "Fear and Self-Loathing," *New York Times* (19 August 1996), p. 36.
30. Ibid., p. 36.
31. Reed, *Active Faith*, pp. 4, 11.
32. Buchanan, *Right From the Beginning*, p. 6.
33. Reed, *Active Faith*, pp. 109–111.
34. Ibid., p. 111.
35. 1996 Republican Party Platform as released over the Republican World Wide Web site on 13 August 1996, p. 15.
36. The Platform Committee, "2004 Republican Platform: A Safer World and a More Hopeful America," http://msnbcmedia.msn.com/I/msnbc/Sections/News/Politics/Conventions/RNC-2004platform.pdf, p. 86.
37. Ibid., p. 84.
38. Christian Coalition of America, "Our Mission," http://www.cc.org/mission.cfm.
39. Ibid.
40. Christian Coalition, http://cc.org.
41. Ibid.
42. Christian Coalition of America, "Our Mission," http://www.cc.org/mission.cfm.
43. Pam Belluck, "Kansas Votes to Delete Evolution From State's Science Curriculum," *New York Times on the Web*, 12 August 1999. Available: www.nytimes.com
44. Ibid.
45. Ibid.
46. Ibid.

47. Pam Belluck, "Board Decision on Evolution Roils an Election in Kansas," *New York Times on the Web*, 29 July 00. Available: www.nytimes.com.
48. Ibid.
49. Ibid.
50. Ibid.
51. Ibid.
52. Ibid.
53. John W. Fountain, "Kansas Puts Evolution Back Into Public Schools," *New York Times on the Web*, 15 February 2001. Available: www.nytimes.com.
54. Ibid.
55. Ibid.
56. *No Child Left Behind Act of 2001* ..., pp. 556–557.
57. Joan Delfattore, *What Johnny Shouldn't Read: Textbook Censorship in America* (New Haven, CT: Yale University Press, 1992), p. 14.
58. Ibid., pp. 36–60.
59. Ibid., pp. 61–75.
60. Ibid., pp. 76–79.
61. Ibid., p. 81.
62. Ibid., p. 87.
63. Haley Barbour, *Agenda for America: A Republican Direction for the Future* (Washington, DC: Regnery, 1996), p. 159.
64. Reed, *Active Faith*, pp. 117–118.
65. Ibid., p. 118.
66. See Eric Schmitt, "Church Leaders Split on Plan for School Prayer Amendment," *New York Times*, 24 July 1995, p. A16, and Jim Luther, "School Prayer," *Compuserve Executive News Service, Associated Press*, 22 July 1996, p. 1.
67. Schmitt, "Church Leaders," p. 16.
68. Ibid.
69. U.S. Department of Education, "Guidance on Constitutionally Protected Prayer in Public Elementary and Secondary Schools (February 7, 2003)," http://www.ed.gov/policy/gen/guid/religionandschools/prayer_guidance.html.
70. Ibid.
71. Buchanan, *Right From the Beginning*, p. 339; Reed, *Active Faith*, p. 131.
72. The Platform Committee, "2004 Republican Platform ...," p. 83.
73. *No Child Left Behind* ..., p. 558.
74. The Platform Committee, "2004 Republican Platform ...," p. 85.
75. Ibid., p. 86.
76. *No Child Left Behind* ..., p. 262.
77. The Platform Committee, "2004 Republican Platform ...," p. 86.
78. *No Child Left Behind* ..., p. 557.
79. Laurie Asseso, "Teen Chastity," *Compuserve Executive News Service*, No. 2120, (17 February 1991).
80. Buchanan, *Right From the Beginning*, p. 339; Reed, *Active Faith*, p. 131.
81. Reed, *Active Faith*, pp. 229–231.
82. Ibid., p. 234.
83. See Joel Spring, *The American School 1642–2004 Sixth Edition* (New York: McGraw-Hill, 2005), pp. 168–206.

84. Bennett, *The De-Valuing of America*, p. 170.
85. Ibid.
86. Karen Diegmuller, "Removal of Literary Works From California Test Stirs Flap," *Education Week*, 9 March 1994, 11.
87. Karen Diegmuller, "Model Exam in California Is Target of New Attacks," *Education Week*, 4 May 1994, 1, 12.
88. 1996 Republican Platform, p. 21.
89. Ibid.
90. Ibid., p. 17.
91. Bennett, *The De-Valuing of America*, p. 26.

CHAPTER 2

1. *No Child Left Behind Act of 2001, Public Law 107-110* (January 8, 2002) http://www.ed.gov/policy/elsec/leg/esea02/107-110.pdf, p. 35.
2. Murray N. Rothbard, *Man, Economy, and State: A Treatise of Economic Principles* (Los Angeles: Nash, 1970).
3. See Peter Boettke, "Friedrich A. Hayek (1899–1992)," Department of Economics, New York University. Available: www.econ.nyu.edu/user/boettke/hayek.htm, p. 1. Unpublished manuscript.
4. Friedrich Hayek, *The Road to Serfdom* (Chicago: University of Chicago Press, 1994).
5. Milton Friedman, *Capital and Freedom* (Chicago: University of Chicago Press, 1962), p. 89.
6. Ibid., p. 92.
7. James Smith, *The Idea Brokers and the Rise of the New Policy Elite* (New York: The Free Press, 1991), p. 181.
8. William Simon, *A Time for Truth* (New York: Readers Digest Press, 1978), p. 233.
9. Ibid., p. xii.
10. Ibid.
11. Ibid., pp. 232–233.
12. Ibid., p. 230.
13. Smith, *The Idea Brokers*, p. 182.
14. David M. Ricci, *The Transformation of American Politics: The New Washington and the Rise of Think Tanks* (New Haven, CT: Yale University Press, 1993), p. 166.
15. "Manhattan Institute for Policy Research," Manhattan Institute Web site, http:// www.manhattan-institute.org/.
16. "About the Center for Civic Innovation at the Manhattan Institute: Educational Reform," http://www.manhattan-institute.org/html/cci.htm#02.
17. "About Manhattan Institute," Manhattan Institute Web site, http://www.manhattan-institute.org.
18. Ibid.
19. "Sponsoring the Manhattan Institute," Manhattan Institute Web site, http://www. manhattan-institute.org.
20. Ibid.
21. Edward Wyatt, "Floyd Flake to Take Post With Education Company," The New York Times on the Web, 3 May 2000.

22. "Program Areas: Educational Reform," Manhattan Institute Web site, http://www. manhattan-institute.org.

23. Republican National Committee, "Education and Opportunity: Leave No American Behind," Republican National Platform. Available: www.rnc.org/2000/2000platform3.

24. "An Evaluation of the Florida A-Plus Accountability and School Choice," Manhattan Institute Web site, http://www.manhattan-institute.org.

25. Jeb Bush, "Civic Bulletin 22: Achievement and Opportunity: Keys to Quality Education." Available: http://www.manhattan-institute.org.

26. "Program Areas: Educational Reform," Manhattan Institute Web site, http://www. manhattan-institute.org.

27. Ibid.

28. Steven Greenhouse, "Autumn of Teachers' Discontent Is Dawning," The New York Times on the Web, 20 September 2000. Available: www.nytimes.com.

29. Jacques Steinberg, "Blue Books Closed, Students Protest State Tests," The New York Times on the Web, 13 April 2000. Available: www.nytimes.com.

30. Jodi Wilogoren, "Seeking to Clone Schools of Success for Poor," The New York Times on the Web, 16 August 2000. Available: www.nytimes.com.

31. "Who's Who at CUNY," The New York Times on the Web, 6 May 1998. Available: www.nytimes.com.

32. Michael Lind, *Up From Conservatism: Why the Right Is Wrong for America* (New York: The Free Press, 1996), p. 182.

33. Lind, *Up From Conservatism*, p. 197.

34. Richard J. Herrnstein & Charles Murray, *The Bell Curve: Intelligence and Class Structure in American Life* (New York: The Free Press, 1994), p. 562.

35. Ibid., p. 562.

36. Ibid., p. 418.

37. Ibid., p. 441.

38. Chester Finn, Jr. describes the development of the Educational Excellence Network in Chester Finn, Jr., "Farewell—and Hello Again (Finn's Last Stand)," Thomas Fordham Foundation Website, http://www.edexcellence .net/foundation/publication/publication.cfm?id=188.

39. Chester Finn, Jr., "Farewell—and Hello Again (Finn's Last Stand), December 1996," *Network News & Views*, http://www.edexcellence.net/foundation/publication/publication.cfm?id=188.

40. "History," http://www.edexcellence.net/foundation/global/page.cfm?id=10.

41. "Mission," http://www.edexcellence.net.

42. Fordham Foundation, "Mission," http://www.edexcellence.net/foundation/global/page.cfm?id=6.

43. See http://www.edexcellence.net.

44. Ibid.

45. Hudson Institute Web site: http://www.al.com/hudson/.

46. Chester Finn, Jr., "Beating Up on Charter Schools," *The New York Times*, 24 August 1996, p. A23.

47. "Chester E. Finn, Jr. Biographical Summary." Available: http://www. edexcellence.net.

48. "Diane Ravitch Biographical Summary." Available: http://www. edexcellence.net.

49. See http://www.nynetworks.org/home.

50. Biographical summaries of Chester Finn, Jr. and Diane Ravitch can be found at http://www.edexcellence.net.
51. Chester Finn, Jr., "Education Without the State 7/10/96." Available: http://www.edexcellence.net.
52. See Diane Ravitch, *The Troubled Crusade: American Education 1945–1980* (New York: Basic Books, 1983).
53. Chester Finn, Jr., & Diane Ravitch, "Educational Reform 1995–96. Part V: Reforming the Federal Role." Available: http://www.edexcellence.net, p. 6.
54. Ibid., p. 7.
55. Ibid., p. 7.
56. Grace Smith, "What Parents Should Know for Back to School," *WebMemo #561(September 3, 2004), Heritage Foundation*, www.heritage.org, p. 1.
57. "No Child Left Behind: Mend It, End It, or Let It Work?" American Enterprise Institute, http://www.aei.org/events/eventID.878,filter./event_detail.asp.
58. "Summary: No Child Left Behind: Mend It, End It, or Let It Work?" American Enterprise Institute, http://www.aei.org/events/eventID.878,filter./event_detail.asp.
59. Ibid.
60. Smith, *The Idea Brokers*, p. 197.
61. Ibid., pp. 197–202.
62. Chester E. Finn & Diane Ravitch, "Magna Charter? A Report Card on School Reform in 1995," Policy Review (Fall 1995): p. 74; Dinesh D'Souza, "We the Slaveowners: In Jefferson's America, Were Some Men Not Created Equal?", Policy Review (Fall 1995): p. 74.
63. D'Souza, "We the Slaveowners," p. 21.
64. Dinesh D'Souza, *Illiberal Education: The Politics of Race and Sex on Campus* (New York: Vintage Books, 1992); Dinesh D'Souza, *The End of Racism* (New York: The Free Press, 1995).
65. Ibid., p. 42.
66. Matthew Spalding, "Character and the Destiny of Free Government," *Building A Culture of Character, Heritage Lectures* (Washington, DC: The Heritage Foundation, 2002).
67. Ibid.
68. Joseph Loconte, "The Importance of Believing in Charity (July 7, 2003)," http://www.heritage.org/Press/Commentary/ed070703a.cfm?Renderfor Print=1.
69. Quoted in Smith, *The Idea Brokers*, p. 178.
70. Peter Brimelow, *Alien Nation: Common Sense About America's Immigration Disaster* (New York: HarperPerennial, 1996), p. 278.
71. Ibid.
72. Ibid., pp. 301–305.
73. Ibid., p. 264.
74. Ibid., pp. 264–265.
75. Chester Finn, Jr., & Diane Ravitch, "Educational Reform 1995–96 Introduction." Available: www.edexcellence.net, p. 2.

76. National Commission on Excellence in Education, *A Nation at Risk: The Imperatives for Educational Reform* (Washington, DC: Department of Education, 1983), p. 5.
77. National Manpower Council, *Student Deferment and National Manpower Policy* (New York: Columbia University Press, 1951), pp. 8–9.
78. National Manpower Council, *A Policy for Scientific and Professional Manpower* (New York: Columbia University Press, 1953).
79. Dwight D. Eisenhower, "Our Future Security," in *Science and Education for National Defense: Hearings Before the Committee on Labor and Public Welfare, United States Senate, Eighty-Fifth Congress, Second Session* (Washington, DC: U.S. Government Printing Office, 1958), p. 1360.
80. See Joel Spring, *The Sorting Machine Revisited: National Educational Policy Since 1945*, rev. ed. (White Plains, NY: Longman, 1989), pp. 151–155.
81. Task Force on Teaching as a Profession, *A Nation Prepared: Teachers for the 21st Century* (New York: Carnegie Corporation, 1986).
82. Task Force on Education for Economic Growth, *Action for Excellence* (Denver, CO: Education Commission of the States, 1983), p. 18.
83. Louis Gerstner, Jr., with Roger D. Semerad, Denis Philip Doyle, & William Johnston, *Reinventing Education: Entrepreneurship in America's Public Schools* (New York: Dutton, 1994), p. ix.
84. Ibid., pp. ix–x.
85. Millicent Lawton, "Summit Accord Calls for Focus on Standards," *Education Week*, 3 April 1996, pp. 1, 14–15.
86. See Ann Bradley, "Pioneers in Professionalism," *Education Week*, 20 April 1993, pp. 19–20, 24.
87. Lind, *Up From Conservatism*, p. 199.
88. David C. Berliner & Bruce Biddle, *The Manufactured Crisis: Myths, Fraud, and the Attack on America's Public Schools* (New York: Addison-Wesley, 1995).
89. The President's Education Summit With Governors: Joint Statement, *America 2000: An Education Strategy* (Washington, DC: U.S. Government Printing Office, 1991), p. 73.
90. Ibid.
91. The President's Education Summit With Governors: Joint Statement, *Remarks by the President at the Presentation of the National Education Strategy* (Washington, DC: U.S. Government Printing Office), pp. 1–2.
92. Ibid.
93. The President's Education Summit With Governors: Joint Statement, *For Today's Students: Better and More Accountable Schools* (Washington, DC: U.S. Government Printing Office), p. 21.
94. Ibid.
95. Jonathan Weisman, "Educators Watch With a Wary Eye as Business Gains Policy Muscle," *Education Week*, 31 July 1991, p. 25.
96. Spring, *The Sorting Machine*, pp. 80–85.
97. *No Child Left Behind Act of 2001, Public Law 107-110* (January 8, 2002) http://www.ed.gov/policy/elsec/leg/esea02/107-110.pdf, p. 243.

98. Catherine Cornbleth & Dexter Waugh, *The Great Speckled Bird: Multicultural Politics and Education Policymaking* (Mahwah, NJ: Lawrence Erlbaum Associates, 1995), pp. 16–17, 68–71.

99. Ibid., pp. 93–185.

100. Arthur M. Schlesinger, Jr., *The Disuniting of America* (Knoxville, TN: Whittle Direct Books, 1991), p. 8.

101. Quoted in Caroline B. Cody, Arthur Woodward, & David L. Elliot, "Race, Ideology and the Battle Over the Curriculum," in *The New Politics of Race and Gender*, Ed. Catherine Marshall (Washington, DC: Falmer Press, 1993), p. 55.

102. Quoted in Cornbleth & Waugh, *The Great Speckled Bird*, p. 85.

103. Quoted in Cornbleth & Waugh, *The Great Speckled Bird*, p. 65.

104. Quoted in Cornbleth & Waugh, *The Great Speckled Bird*, p. 66.

105. "Plan to Teach U.S. History Is Said to Slight White Males," *New York Times*, 26 October 1994, p. B12.

106. Carol Gluck, "Let the Debate Continue," *New York Times*, 26 October 1994, p. 23.

107. Karen Diegmueller, "Revise History Standards, Two Panels Advise," *Education Week*, 18 October 1995, p. 11.

108. Ibid.

109. Ibid.

110. Karen Diegmueller, "History Center Shares New Set of Standards," *Education Week*, 10 April 1996, p. 1.

111. Diane Ravitch, *A Consumer's Guide to High School History Textbooks* (Washington, DC: Fordham Institute, 2004).

112. *No Child Left Behind ...*, p. 33.

113. Ibid., p. 42.

114. Ibid., p. 35.

115. Ibid., p. 58.

116. Ibid., p. 122.

117. Ibid., pp. 58, 70, 122, 185, 201, 206, 219, 232, 248, 297, 382, 419, 584, 657.

118. Ibid., p. 376.

119. Ibid., p. 55.

120. Ibid., p. 61.

121. Ibid., p. 187.

122. Ibid., p. 364.

123. Schlesinger, *The Disuniting of America*, p. 8.

124. James Traub, "Has Benno Schmidt Learned His Lesson?", *New York Times*, 31 October 1994, pp. 51–59.

125. Ibid.

126. Ibid., p. 58.

127. Chester Finn, Jr., Bruno V. Manno, & Louann A. Bierlein, "Section 5: Conclusions and Recommendations," in *Charter Schools in Action: What Have We Learned?* (Indianapolis, IN: Hudson Institute, 1996), p. 5.

128. The Platform Committee, "2004 Republican Platform: A Safer World and a More Hopeful America," http://msnbcmedia.msn.com/I/msnbc/Sections/News/Politics/Conventions/RNC-2004platform.pdf, p. 56.

129. "Edison Charter Schools," http://www.edisonschools.com/overview/charter.html.

130. "Company Profile," http://www.edisonschools.com/overview/ov0.html.
131. Quoted in Smith, *The Idea Brokers*, p. 20.

CHAPTER 3

1. Democratic Leadership Council, "How a 21st Century Party Can Promote 21st Century Jobs, Panel II: Creating Higher-Skill, Higher-Wage Jobs, Democratic National Convention, Boston, Massachusetts (July 28, 2004), http://www.ndol.org/print.cfm?contentid=252833.
2. Ibid.
3. Platform Standing Committee, *Report of the Platform Committee: Strong at Home, Respected in the World, The Democratic Platform for America* (Boston: 2004 Democratic National Convention, 2004), p. 30.
4. Paul Weinstein, Jr., and Eben Gilfenbaum, "Head to Head on the Issues" *Blueprint Magazine*, Vol. 2004 No. 4 (October 7, 2004) http://www.ndol.org/print.cfm?contentid=252935.
5. "About the Democratic Leadership Council," http://www.ndol.org/ndol_ci.cfm?kaid=86&subid=85&contentid=893.
6. "About The Progressive Policy Institute," http://www.ppionline.org/ppi_ci.cfm?knlgAreaID=87&subsecID=205&contentID=896.
7. John Hale, "The People Behind the Ideas at the Progressive Policy Institute," Democratic Leadership Council home page, http://www.dlcppi.com.
8. Ted Kolderie, "Beyond Choice to New Public Schools: Withdrawing the Exclusive Franchise in Public Education," Policy Report, November 1990, No. 8, 3. Available: http://www.dlcppi.com.
9. Ibid., p. 13.
10. Democratic Leadership Council and the Progressive Policy Institute, "The New Progressive Declaration: A Political Philosophy for the Information Age (July 10, 1996), *http://www.ndol.org/print.cfm?contentid=839*.
11. Ibid., p. 1.
12. Ibid., p. 2.
13. Platform Standing Committee, *Report of the Platform Committee: Strong at Home, Respected in the World, The Democratic Platform for America*, p. 30.
14. Democratic Leadership Council and the Progressive Policy Institute, "The New Progressive Declaration, p. 2.
15. Ibid., p. 3.
16. Ibid., p. 2.
17. Meredith L. Oakley, *On the Make: The Rise of Bill Clinton* (Washington, DC: Regnery, 1994), p. 275.
18. Ibid., p. 277.
19. Ibid., p. 287.
20. Ibid., p. 291.
21. Jacob Weisberg, *In Defense of Government: The Fall and Rise of Public Trust* (New York: Scribner's, 1996), p. 132.
22. Bill Clinton & Al Gore, *Putting People First: How We Can All Change America* (New York: Times Books, 1992), p. 3.
23. The Report of the Platform Committee to the 1996 Democratic National Convention, The 1996 Democratic National Platform (1996), p. 1.

24. Ibid.
25. Hillary Rodham Clinton, *It Takes a Village and Other Lessons Children Teach Us* (New York: Simon & Schuster, 1996), p. 312.
26. Ibid., p. 308.
27. Ibid., p. 307.
28. Bill Clinton, *Between Hope and History: Meeting America's Challenges for the 21st Century* (New York: Times Books, 1996), pp. 6–7.
29. Ibid., p. 7.
30. Clinton & Gore, *Putting People First*, p. 86.
31. Ibid., p. 85.
32. "Clinton's Speech Accepting the Democratic Nomination for President," *New York Times*, 30 August 1996, p. A20.
33. Ibid.
34. Ibid.
35. Bill Clinton, *Between Hope and History*, p. 29.
36. Hillary Clinton, *It Takes a Village*, p. 294.
37. Robert Reich, *The Work of Nations: Preparing Ourselves for 21st-Century Capitalism* (New York: Knopf, 1991), p. 173.
38. Ibid., p. 208.
39. Ibid., pp. 268–300.
40. Ibid., p. 281.
41. Ibid., pp. 261–300.
42. Bill Clinton, *Between Hope and History*, p. 60.
43. Ibid., p. 51.
44. Hillary Clinton, *It Takes a Village*, p. 301.
45. Ibid., p. 300.
46. 1996 Democratic National Platform, p. 12.
47. Bill Clinton, *Between Hope and History*, p. 42.
48. Lynn Olson, "President Signs a School-to-Work Act," *Education Week*, 11 May 1994, pp. 1, 21.
49. Marshall S. Smith, "Education Reform in America's Public Schools: The Clinton Agenda," in Diane Ravitch (Ed.), *Debating the Future of American Education: Do We Need National Standards and Assessments?* (Washington, DC: Brookings Institution, 1995), p. 9.
50. Ibid., p. 10.
51. Ibid., p. 23.
52. Smith, Education Reform, 40. The legislation is quoted by Andrew Porter, "The Uses and Misuses of Opportunity-to-Learn Standards" in Ravitch (Ed.), *Debating the Future of American Education: Do We Need National Standards and Assessments?* (Washington, DC: Brookings Institution, 1995), p. 41.
53. As an example of how long the attempt has been made in the courts to achieve equality of spending between school districts, check Richard Lehne's now-dated book, *The Quest for Justice: The Politics of School Finance Reform* (New York: Longman, 1978). Jonathan Kozol's *Savage Inequalities: Children in America's Schools* (New York: Crown, 1991) is still the best denunciation of the lack of opportunity to learn in many U.S. schools.
54. Porter, "The Uses and Misuses," p. 41.
55. 1996 Democratic National Platform, p. 8.

56. Descriptions and justifications of these programs can be found in Bill Clinton, *Between Hope and History*, pp. 43–52, and the 1996 Democratic National Platform, pp. 7–9.
57. Weisberg, *In Defense of Government*, p. 133.
58. David Osborne & Ted Gaebler, *Reinventing Government: How the Entrepreneurial Spirit Is Transforming the Public Sector* (New York: Penguin, 1993).
59. The 1996 Democratic National Platform, pp. 1, 4.
60. Hale, "The Making of the New Democrats," p. 3.
61. Osborne & Gaebler, *Reinventing Government*, pp. 11–12.
62. Ibid., p. 315.
63. Ibid., p. 316.
64. Ibid., p. 7.
65. The 1996 Democratic National Platform, p. 6.
66. Hillary Clinton, *It Takes a Village*, p. 263.
67. The 1996 Democratic National Platform, p. 7.
68. "A Transcript of the First Televised Debate Between Clinton and Dole," *New York Times*, 7 October 1996, p. B10.
69. Paul Basken, "Clinton Talking Education in California," United Press International, Compuserve, Executive News Service, 12 September 1996, p. 1.
70. "The Gore Agenda: Revolutionizing American Education in the 21st Century." Available: http://www.gore2000.org.
71. "2000 Democratic National Platform," *New York Times* on the Web, 17 August 2000, p. 7. Available: www.nytimes.com
72. Ibid.
73. PPI Project Description (June 29, 2000), "About PPI's 21st Century Schools Project," http://www.ppionline.org/ppi_ci.cfm?contentid=1125&knlgArea ID=110&subsecid=204.
74. Ibid.
75. Ibid.
76. PPI Press Release, December 12, 2001, "Education Reform Legislation Reflects Ideas Proposed by PPI," http://www.ndol.org/print.cfm?contentid= 250069.
77. House NDC, Press Release, December 13, 2001, "New Dems Hail Final Approval of Education Bill," http://www.ndol.org/print.cfm?contentid= 250063.
78. Andrew J. Rotherham, "How Bush Stole Education," *Blueprint Magazine* (25 March 2002), http://www.ndol.org/ndol_ci.cfm?contentid=250319&kaid= 110&subid=900023.
79. Ibid.
80. Ibid.
81. PPI Press Release December 12, 2001.
82. Ibid.
83. House NDC, Press Release.
84. Rotherham.
85. Kathy Emery and Susan Ohanian, *Why Is Corporate America Bashing Our Schools?*
(Portsmouth, NH: Heinemann, 2004); Susan Ohanian, *One Size Fits Few: The Folly of Educational Standards* (Portsmouth, NH: Heinemann, 1999); Alfie Kohn,

The Case Against Standardized Testing: Raising the Scores, Ruining the Schools
(Portsmouth, NH: Heinemann, 2000); and Peter Sacks, *Standardized Minds:
The High Price of America's Testing Culture and What We Can Do to Change It* (New
York: Perseus Publishing, 2001).

86. Save Our Schools, http://www.sosvoice.org.
87. "Ten Alarming Facts About No Child Left Behind" (Monday, 26 July 2004),
    http://www.sosvoice.org.
88. John Kerry and John Edwards, *Our Plan for America: Strong at Home, Respected
    in the World* (New York: Public Affairs, 2004), p. 92.
89. John Kerry, *A Call to Service: My Vision for a Better America* (New York: Viking,
    Penguin Group, 2003) p. 104.
90. Platform Standing Committee, *Report of the Platform Committee: Strong at
    Home, Respected in the World, The Democratic Platform for America*, p. 31.
91. Kerry, *A Call to Service*, p. 97.
92. Ibid., p. 97.
93. Platform Standing Committee, *Report of the Platform Committee: Strong at
    Home, Respected in the World, The Democratic Platform for America*, p. 32.
94. Ibid., p. 32.
95. Ibid., p. 22.
96. Ibid., p. 107.
97. Ibid., p. 107.
98. Ibid., pp. 107–108.
99. Ibid., pp. 108–109.
100. Platform Standing Committee, *Report of the Platform Committee: Strong at
     Home, Respected in the World, The Democratic Platform for America*, p. 31.
101. Progressive Policy Institute Press Release (September 8, 2004) "PPI Unveils
     National Strategy to Expand Early Childhood Education, Report Outlines
     Federal-State Partnership to Close Preparation Gap and Foster Accountabil-
     ity," http://www.ppionline.org/ppi_ci.cfm?contentid=252868&knlg
     AreaID=85&subsecid=108.
102. Platform Standing Committee, *Report of the Platform Committee: Strong at
     Home, Respected in the World, The Democratic Platform for America*, p. 31.
103. Ibid., p. 31.
104. Progressive Policy Institute Press Release (September 8, 2004) "PPI Unveils
     National Strategy to Expand Early Childhood Education," p. 3.
105. Ibid., p. 1.
106. Ibid., p. 2.
107. Ibid., p. 3.
108. Ibid., p. 3.
109. See Jennifer Day and Eric Newburger, *The Big Payoff: Educational Attainment
     and Synthetic Estimates of Work-Life Earnings* (Washington, DC: U.S. Bureau of
     the Census, July 2002).
110. Sakiko Fukuda et al., *Human Development Report 2003: Millennium Develop-
     ment Goals: A Compact Among Nations to End Human Poverty* (New York: Oxford
     University Press, 2003), p. 237.
111.See Nicholas D. Kristof, "Where Conformity Rules, Misfits Thrive," *The New
     York Times* (18 May 1997), Section 2, p. 43.

CHAPTER 4

1. In recent years there have been a number of books published on the ideology of consumerism. A good introduction can be found in a series of articles published in Juliet Schor and Douglas Holt (Eds.), *The Consumer Reader* (New York: New Press, 2000).
2. Ralph Nader, "Children and Education." Available: http://votenader.org.
3. Ibid.
4. Ibid.
5. The 1996 Green Platform, "IV. Platform Policy Document: Democracy: B. Political Participation." Available: www.greenparty.org.
6. Ibid.
7. Ralph Nader, "Why Is the Government Protecting Corporations That Prey on Kids?", 22 September, 1999. Available: http://votenader.org.
8. Ibid.
9. Ralph Nader, "Making Parents Irrelevant," 27 October 1999. Available: http:// votenader.org.
10. Nader, "Why Is the Government ... "
11. Ibid.
12. Ibid.
13. Ralph Nader, "Commerce in the Classroom," 12 May 1999. Available: http:// votenader.org.
14. Ibid.
15. Ibid.
16. "Terence R., McAullife's Reply to Ralph Nader (January 23, 2004)," http://www.votenader.org/why_ralph/index.php?cid=8.
17. " Open Reply to Mr. McAuliffe, Chairman of the DNC (June 18, 2004), http://www.votenader.org/why_ralph/materials.php.
18. Brochure distributed by the Nader 2004 campaign: "Let the Debate Begin!" Nader/Camejo 2004, (Paid for by Nader for President 2004 General Election Committee, P.O. Box 18002, Washington, DC 20036).
19. Press Release, "Nader: Iraq an Unconstitutional, Illegal War Based on Five Falsehoods: congress Should Begin Impeachment Inquiry of Bush and Cheney" (April 13, 2004) (Washington, DC: Nader for President 2004).
20. "Equal Access to Education," Campaign material titled *Nader on Education*, http://votenader.org/issues/index.php?cid=36.
21. "Education for Everyone," Campaign material titled *Nader on Education* ....
22. "Equal Access to Education .... "
23. "Education: Over-emphasis on Standardized Testing," Campaign material titled *Nader on Education* ....
24. Ibid.
25. Ibid.
26. "Equal Access to Education .... "
27. Ibid.
28. Ibid.
29. Ibid.
30. *Green Party of the United States: Platform 2004* (Washington DC: Green Party, 2004), p. 28.

31. The 1996 Green Platform, "IV. Platform Policy Document: Democracy: B. Political Participation." Available: www.greenparty.org.
32. *Green Party of the United States: Platform 2004 ...*, p. 7.
33. Ibid., p. 9.
34. Ibid., p. 23.
35. Ibid., p. 23.
36. Ibid., p. 28.
37. Ibid., p. 28.
38. Ibid., p. 28.
39. Ibid., p. 28.
40. Ibid., p. 27.
41. Ibid., p. 28.
42. Ibid., p. 28.
43. Ibid. p. 32.
44. Ibid., p. 37.
45. Ibid., p. 28.
46. Ibid., p. 28.
47. Ibid., p. 28.
48. Ibid., p. 17.
49. Ibid., p. 29.
50. Ibid., p. 29.
51. Ibid., p. 29.
52. Ibid., p. 17.
53. Jacob Weisberg, *In Defense of Government: The Fall and Rise of Public Trust* (New York: Scribner's, 1996), p. 137.
54. See the biographical sketch "Reverend Jesse L. Jackson, Rainbow Founder." Available: www.cais.net/rainbow/, p. 1.
55. Ibid., p. 1.
56. Ibid.
57. Ibid.
58. Ibid., p. 2.
59. The Feminist Majority, "What Is Affirmative Action?" Available: http://www.feminist.org, p. 2.
60. Ibid., pp. 1–3.
61. Jesse Jackson, "Let Them Eat Grits: Pseudo-Intellect Mixes Race, I.Q. to Justify America's Ethnic Cleansing." Available: http://www.cais.net/rainbow/, p. 1.
62. Ibid., p. 2.
63. Ibid.
64. Jesse Jackson, Sr., "How to Keep Hope Alive: The Future of the Rainbow Coalition," Address by the Reverend Jesse L. Jackson, Sr. at the John F. Kennedy Jr. Forum, Harvard University, Institute of Politics, John F. Kennedy School of Government, February 17, 2004, http://www.rainbowpush.org/FMPro?-db=rpodata.fp5&-format=rainbowpush%2fdata%2fdetailspeech.htm&-lay=main&-sortfield=date&-sortorder=descend&category=speech&year=2004&-max=20&-recid=32999&-find=.
65. Ibid.
66. Ibid.
67. Ibid.

68. Ibid.
69. Ibid.
70. Ibid.
71. National Organization for Women, "The Truth About George," http://www.thetruthaboutgeorge.com/.
72. "The National Organization for Women's 1966 Statement of Purpose." Available: http://www.now.org, p. 3.
73. "Statement of NOW President Patricia Ireland as Hundreds Demonstrate at White House Over Welfare." Available: http://www.now.org, p. 1.
74. Ibid., p. 2.
75. "Media Alert: April 14 in San Francisco 500 Progressive Groups Will Unite for the 'Fight the Right' March and Protest March 19, 1996." Available: http://www.now.org, p. 1.
76. "The National Organization for Women's 1966 Statement of Purpose," p. 1.
77. Ibid., p. 1.
78. Ibid., p. 4.
79. Ibid., p. 2.
80. Ibid., p. 5.
81. "NOW Task Force On Education," May 1967. Available: http://www.now.org.
82. "The Feminist Chronicles 1973–1982," www.now.org, 4.
83. Ibid., p. 14.
84. "The Feminist Chronicles 1983–1992." Available: http://www.now.org, p. 4.
85. Ibid.
86. "NOW Leaders Call Supreme Court Decision on VMI A 'Mixed Bag' Victory," 26 June 1996. Available: http://www.now.org, p. 1.
87. Ibid.
88. "Opening Doors in Education." Available: http://www.feminist.org., pp. 1–2.
89. Ibid., p. 3.
90. Ibid.
91. "Feminist Who." Available: http://www.feminist.org, p. 1.
92. National Organization for Women, "Comments of the National Organization for Women on the Department of Education's Notice of Intent to Regulate on Single-Sex Education," http://www.now.org/issues/education/single-sex-education-comments.html.
93. Ibid.
94. Ibid.
95. United States Department of Education, 34 CFR, Part 106, RIN 1870-AA11, "Nondiscrimination on the Basis of Sex in Education Programs or Activities Receiving Federal Financial Assistance," *Federal Register*, (Tuesday, March 9, 2004), (Washington, DC: U. S. Government Printing Office, 2004), Vol. 69, No. 46, p. 11275.
96. Ibid., p. 11276.
97. Ibid., p. 11277.
98. Michael Tomasky, *Left for Dead: The Life, Death and Possible Resurrection of Progressive Politics in America* (New York: The Free Press, 1996), p. 11.
99. Ibid., p. 2.
100. Ibid., p. 196.
101. Ibid., pp. 198–202.
102. Ibid., p. 211.

Author Index

Numbers in parentheses are footnote numbers and indicate that an author's work is referred to, although his or her name may not be cited in the text. Numbers in italic show the page where the complete reference is given.

A

Asseso, L., 23(79), *119*

B

Barbour, H., 19(63), *119*
Basken, P., 80(69), *127*
Belluck, P., 15(43,44,45,46,47),
　　16(48,49,50,51,52), *118, 119*
Bennett, W. J., 6(13,15), 24(84,85),
　　26(91), *117, 120*
Berliner, D. C., 52(88), *123*
Biddle, B., 52(88), *123*
Bierlein, L. A., 61(127), *124*
Boettke, P., 30(3), *120*
Bradley, A., 52(86), *123*
Brimelow, P., 48(70,71,72,73), 49(74),
　　122
Buchanan, P. J., 4(7), 6(12), 10(32),
　　21(71), 23(80), *117, 118, 119*
Bush, G. W., 1(1,2), 3(4), *117*
Bush, J., 36(25), *121*

C

Clinton, H. R., 70(25,26,27), 71(36),
　　74(44,45), 79(66), *126, 127*
Clinton, W. J., 69(22), 70(28,29,30,31),
　　71(35), 74(42,43,47), 77(56),
　　125, 126, 127

Cody, C. B., 55(101), *124*
Cornbleth, C., 55(98,99),
　　56(102,103,104), *124*

D

Day, J., 89(109), *128*
Delfattore, J., 17(57), 18(58,59,60,61),
　　19(62), *119*
Diegmuller, K., 25(86,87),
　　57(107,108,109,110), *120, 124*
Doyle, D. P., 51(83,84), *123*
D'Souza, D., 46(63,64,65), *122*

E

Edwards, J., 85(88), *128*
Eisenhower, D. D., 50(79), *123*
Elliot, D. L., 55(101), *124*
Emery, K., 83(85), *127*

F

Finn, C., Jr., 41(38,39), 43(46),
　　44(51,53,54,55), 46(62), 49(75),
　　61(127), *121, 122, 124*
Fountain, J. W., 16(53,54), 17(55), *119*
Friedman, M., 31(5,6), *120*
Fukuda, S., 89(110), *128*

133

Subject Index

A

Abortion
  NOW and, 110
  Republican party platform and, 11–12
Abrams, Steve, 15
Abstinence, compassionate conservatives on, 21
Access to education, New Democrats and, 75–76
Accountability
  in Goals 2000, 54
  New Democrats and, 81–83, 88
Action for Excellence, 51
Affirmative action, 9
  neoconservatives on, 38–39, 46, 48–49
  NOW on, 108–110
  Rainbow Coalition on, 103–104
Alexander, Lamar, 51, 53, 68–69
America 2000: An Education Strategy, 53
American Civil Liberties Union, 18, 22–23
American Enterprise Institute, 33, 37, 45–49
American Family Assocation, 17–18
American Federation of Teachers, *see* Teachers' unions
Americans United for Separation of Church and State, 20
Armey, Dick, 19
Art education, Green Party and, 101–102
Asner, Ed, 16

Austrian economics, 70
  versus neoconservatism, 51

B

Babbit, Joel, 94
Back-To-School Pledge, 105
Barbour, Haley, 19
Baroody, William J., 47–48
Bayh, Evan, 82
The Bell Curve (Herrnstein & Murray), 34, 37–39, 48, 104
Bennett, William, 6, 24, 26, 43, 57
Berliner, David, 52
Biddle, Bruce, 52
Bierlein, Louann, 61
Bilingual Education Act, 23–24
  neoconservatives on, 44, 48–49
Bork, Robert, 48
Boy Scouts of America, 22
Brimelow, Peter, 48
Brown, Mary Douglass, 16
Brownback, Sam, 15
Buchanan, Pat, 4, 6, 10, 21, 46
Buckley, William F., 48
Bureacracy, neoconservatism on, 30
Burke, Edmund, 13
Bush, George H. W., 43, 52–54
Bush, George W.
  on compassionate conservatism, 3
  influences on, 3–5, 34–39
  Jackson on, 105–106
  Nader and, 97

137